MANTRIC SAYINGS

MEDITATIONS

1903–1925

RUDOLF STEINER (1916)

MANTRIC SAYINGS
MEDITATIONS
1903–1925

TRANSLATED BY DANA L. FLEMING
AND CHRISTOPHER BAMFORD

INTRODUCTION BY CHRISTOPHER BAMFORD

RUDOLF STEINER

SteinerBooks

CW 268

This book is supported by a gift in memory of
HARVEY AND LOUISE LISLE

* * *

SteinerBooks
Anthropsophic Press

610 Main Street
Great Barrington, Massachusetts 01230
www.steinerbooks.org

Translated by Dana L. Fleming and Christopher Bamford

This book is volume 268 in the Collected Works (CW) of Rudolf Steiner, published by SteinerBooks, 2015. It is a translation of *Mantrische Spruche. Seelenübungen II 1903-1925,* published by Rudolf Steiner Verlag, Dornach, Switzerland, 1999.

Print ISBN: 978-0-88010-630-6
eBook ISBN: 978-1-62148-078-5

CONTENTS

One would have to write many books if one wished to exhaust the whole meaning of these sayings, for not only is every word in them filled with meaning, but also the symmetry of the words, the way in which they are distributed, the intensifications that they contain, and many other things, are also filled with meaning, so that only long and patient dedication to what lies within them can begin to exhaust them.

Rudolf Steiner, 1907, CW 284

Sayings such as these do not arise arbitrarily from some personality, but are taken from the spiritual world. Much more is contained in them than people usually think. People think about them in the right way, therefore, when they assume that they will never wholly fathom them, but that the more they deepen themselves in them, the more they will find.

Rudolf Steiner, October, 24, 1905, CW 266/1

I notice that such sayings have the characteristic that the purely grammatical structure sometimes presents difficulties. These difficulties, however, are given by the spiritual world for the ends that they ought to serve.

Rudolf Steiner, January 19, 1915, CW 157

INTRODUCTION

Attention is the purest form of generosity.

SIMONE WEIL (Letter to Jöe Bousquet)

The kingdom of heaven is like a mustard seed
which a man took and planted in his field. Though
it is the smallest of all seeds, yet when it grows,
it is the largest of plants and becomes a tree,
so that the birds come and perch in its branches.

MATTHEW 13, 31-32

Transform yourself for the sake of the world. Learn to practice thinking, feeling, sensing, and willing without egotism. Let the spirit see through you, create through you: Learn to sacrifice the self for the Self: to live and work out of the spirit. Become the stage on which the eternal and the transitory meet, an organ of cognition for the eternal, so that you become the eye and the hand of the spirit. "Let your work be the shadow that your I casts / when it is shone upon by the flame of your higher self." Always remember: "without faith, the work remains dead." "Understand: that you should divinize yourself through your meditation."

With such injunctive insights this unique collection of Rudolf Steiner's mantric sayings, the companion volume to *Soul Exercises: Word and Symbol Meditations* (CW 267) opens.

By "mantric sayings" (*Mantrische Sprüche*), Rudolf Steiner means content given by the spiritual world to be absorbed and experienced in meditation. Thus the volume contains intuitive insights—sometimes in sentences, sometimes in "verse" form—received "from the spiritual world," and as such, the vehicle to return us to it. The meditations were often given personally to others for general use, as well as for specific situations or needs, such as healing and strengthening, or in relation to those who have died, or for anthroposophic work. There are also translations of certain scriptural passages and ancient versions of the Lord's Prayer, which were part of Steiner's own meditative practice. As he often advised, sentences from sacred texts, as well as from the mystics, derive from the spiritual world, and are intended and most appropriate for our meditations. The volume also contains the lecture "The Foundation Stone Address" of 1913, for this, too, contains gifts of the spirit—above all, the so-called "Macrocosmic (or Reverse) Lord's Prayer."

In other words, these are short texts intended for meditation, received meditatively. That is, they are not texts whose primary function is to communicate information of some kind. Rather, they are to be performed: to be experienced. In this sense, they are both injunctive, enjoining us to "Do this!", and affirmative, positive, filled with hope, and oriented toward the other, the future.

In this regard, it is interesting to note that an alternative translation of *Sprüche* or "sayings" is "aphorisms," a term not infrequently invoked by Rudolf Steiner for certain kinds of short texts. Often we think of aphorisms as simply smart, pithy, laconic sayings, but, since Nietzsche made aphorisms the basis of his philosophical style (which Steiner deeply appreciated), an aphorism can mean a form of intense, concentrated, sometimes paradoxical or counter-intuitive expression, oriented toward the spirit with the capacity to move and affect us beyond its propositional value, and creating a receptivity toward what might come and a line of flight to follow it. Many of Jesus' "sayings," such as those of the Sermon on the Mount (rendered by Steiner in this volume) are of this kind.

A little like Zen koans, such aphorisms confront us with something that our ordinary thinking cannot quite grasp, so that we are forced to abandon it and a different kind of consciousness, another mode of cognition, can take its place. In this vein, for instance, Rudolf Steiner proposes for meditation such powerful mantras as "It thinks me" or "It works me." This aphoristic, consciousness-transforming quality, in fact, is why such verses or sentences are called "mantric."

The word "mantric" derives from the Sanskrit, *mantra*, which is made up of two words: "man," in its simplest form meaning "to think" or "mind," and "tra," connoting instrumentality or function. A mantra is thus what sets mind in action toward the highest function of what mind can do. For Vedic humanity, however, "man" or mind was more than simply cognitive in the narrow sense; it also included feeling, affect, sensation, will, intention, and even "heart-impulses." Beyond this, it also included the sense of "evoking, calling up." As J. Gonda sums it up:

> A mantra may therefore etymologically speaking, and judging from the oldest texts, approximately be defined as follows: 'Words believed to be of 'superhuman origin,' received fashioned and spoken by the 'inspired' seers, poets, and reciters in order to evoke divine power(s) and especially conceived as a means of creating, conveying, concentrating, and realizing intentional and efficient thought, and of coming into touch or identifying oneself with the essence of divinity, which is present in the mantra. ("The Indian Mantra," *Oriens,* vol. 16, December 1963)

Given the profound transformations of consciousness since Vedic times, it is perhaps surprising that this "definition" is still more or less descriptive of Rudolf Steiner's meaning.

Of course, since meditation lies at the very heart of Anthroposophy as Rudolf Steiner wished to see it practiced, there are many other volumes and collections of Steiner's meditation texts. What makes *Mantric Sayings* unique, however, is its range, extending from July 1903 to March 1925—virtually the entirety of Rudolf Steiner's life as a spiritual teacher—and its personal quality. That is, it is very clear that many of these meditations, whether given to others or simply written in his notebooks or on loose note sheets, were meditations that Rudolf himself not only received, but also worked with himself in meditation. Rudolf Steiner, after all, it is well-known, claimed never to speak, or teach, or write anything that he had not experienced himself. It should come as no surprise, then, that this is also true of the meditations he gave. In this sense, these meditations present a kind of intimate soul-portrait of the one who gave them. They are what he did. At the same time, of course, most of these meditations were subsequently given to others with, as one might imagine, great love and deep knowledge of the recipients.

This quality of personal experience, of course, characterizes all that Rudolf Steiner wrote and spoke regarding meditation. The apparently different approaches outlined in *How to Know High Worlds*, in the relevant chapters of *Theosophy* and *Esoteric Science*, and in the various lectures on different aspects of meditation, all likewise arise from Rudolf Steiner's own experience. For, in the course of his thinking, meditating, researching, and self-schooling, he had done and experienced many things, and would instruct students differently according to need and context as he understood it.

Because it might seem to propose different 'kinds" of meditation, this wide range of approaches and practices could lead to confusion. However, though there are many different kinds—for instance, exercises, often entailing visualizations or the building up of images; aphoristic sentences or phrases; and verses usually in the form of evocations, affirmations, or prayers—all of these depend on or require more or less the same approach: humbly, selflessly, in a mood of reverence and devotion, quieting and stilling the mind or soul, and thus, peaceful, emptied of the inner turmoil of the day, placing within one's consciousness the given meditation or prayer (Rudolf Steiner says that, for early Christians, prayer *was* meditation), pondering it, slowly penetrating it, allowing it to fill one's thinking, feeling, and willing; and then holding this state, living within it as long as possible and then letting it go and returning to one's initial, empty, peaceful state.

*

Given, then, the primacy of meditation for Rudolf Steiner's understanding of anthroposophical practice, and that the meditations he gave were those he did (and hence indicate the nature of his own practice), a brief look at Rudolf Steiner's own path to meditation will perhaps be useful. After all, Rudolf Steiner was always insistent that what he taught—Anthroposophy—should never be separated from his name, his individuality. In this sense, his transformation from "Steiner Rudolf," as he was called as a child, to the "Rudolf Steiner" we know as the spiritual teacher is an important part of the mystery of Anthroposophy, the source of which may be the spirit but whose vessel and expression is the individuality of Rudolf Steiner. However one considers it, it is astounding to contemplate the fact that at the age of forty, within a year of uniting his life with Theosophy, Rudolf Steiner was able not only to speak from experience of the deepest human and cosmic realities, but also to become a unique and flawless teacher of meditation and spiritual practice for others. How he was able to do so is not an idle question; it can help us understand what he sought to instill. If we are to follow in his footsteps, however humbly, a glimpse of his path of development could be an aid in doing so. Though his spiritual unfolding and his life were unique to him, we may always in small ways find echoes and new inspiration in our own life.

To begin with, then, we may note that, while from his childhood the reality of the spiritual world was a self-evident reality and experience, the task of transforming, appropriating, and integrating this gift into a fully human conscious path of inner, spiritual development and research would take many (indeed, almost thirty) years of struggle and constantly metamorphosing practice before he was fully prepared and able to teach what he had experienced. Unlike most "spiritual teachers," Rudolf Steiner himself had no single, clearly identifiable teacher. We may say therefore that he was self-taught, and attribute this to his independence, his deep sense of individuality, and his need and ability to think for himself—freely, as his father, too, had been a "freethinker." But this would be only half true. For we may surmise the consequence of previous incarnations; and we may say, further, that he was taught by the spiritual world—including discarnate teachers such as Christian Rosenkreutz and, after a certain point, Jesus and the Christ. Finally we may point to life itself—embraced and lived ethically as service with complete freedom, and love for others and the world, including thereby profound relationships with many people, named and unnamed, through which he learned much and was much transformed.

His own account in his *Autobiography* makes clear the broad outlines of his trajectory, marked by an innate call to know and a passion for reality. Put another way, we may call it a soul quality of unshakeable devotion and dedication to the truth, which he knew from the beginning to be spiritual, and hence at odds with the dominant culture of materialism into which he was born. These characteristics were coupled with the gift of a natural propensity for reverence and humility, which meant that in some sense he never saw himself as exceptional, or better than anyone else. What he sought and found he always believed was available to all who would make the effort.

In this way, early, spontaneous experiences of the presences of the dead and the beings and forces of nature (which were as real to him as outer, sensory experiences, and which he continued to transform throughout his life), as well as a significant, though brief, awakening to the Christian Mystery as an altar boy—enhanced by the presence of monks from a neighboring monastery whose enigmatic being sparked his interest—led almost seamlessly to the discovery of geometry and the experience of a "soul-space" where he was able to experience "thoughts themselves" and witness spiritual beings and events. This, in turn, then led quite naturally to the need to develop the deep, necessarily meditative thinking required to grasp and penetrate the cognitive paths of Kant, Fichte, Hegel, Schelling, Nietzsche, and above all, Goethe.

All these revolutionary thinkers, whom he took as teachers, demanded intense, sustained, and selfless thinking to penetrate. After all, his interest was by no means academic. It was not simple understanding that he was after. His aim was to grasp the secret thread that united these thinkers, so that he could make it his own and transform it into an adequate doorway not only for himself, but also for, and to, the future. In this, we may say, that he already presciently if inchoately understood that the great labor of thinking and feeling—we may call it "Romanticism"—that had taken place around the turn of the nineteenth century was, in fact, the earthly reflection of the Michael School in the heavens—the fore-stage of the Michael Age, about to begin in 1879. Important here, too, was Steiner's intuitive conviction of the spiritual reality and freedom of the "I." Confirmed in this by his studies of Fichte, the inner conviction gradually grew in him that freedom and love had to be combined on the path toward its conscious realization. Nor should we forget his meeting with the mystical hermetist herb gatherer and teacher of traditional nature wisdom, Felix Kogutski, who introduced him as a practitioner to the work of Paracelsus, Boehme, and the alchemical philosophers; nor the unknown M(aster), perhaps Christian Rosenkreutz, whose "emissary" Kogutski was, and who advised him to take Fichte as his guide in seeking a path toward the transformation of materialist science into a spiritual science. Opening Fichte's *The Science of Knowledge*, Steiner would have found the following prophetic injunction:

> Attend to yourself: turn your attention away from everything that surrounds you and to your inner life; this is the first demand that philosophy makes of its disciple. Our concern is not with anything that lies outside you, but only with yourself. (J.G. Fichte, *The Science of Knowledge*)

This clear call to "meditation" then continues:

> Even the most cursory glance will reveal to anyone a remarkable difference between the various immediate modifications of consciousness, or what we may call our presentations. Some appear to us as completely dependent on our freedom... Others refer to a reality which we take to be established independently of us...In brief, we may say some of our presentations are accompanied by a feeling of freedom, others by a feeling of necessity...
>
> The question, "What is the source of the presentations which are accompanied by the feeling of necessity, and of this feeling of necessity itself?" is one that is surely worthy of reflection.... (J.G. Fichte, ibid.)

Thus, though a work of philosophy, Fichte's *Science of Knowledge* also provides a directive for life. To seek the ground of experience the student is led on a rigorous course of training. Experience is the experience of something by someone. There is a subject and an object: an I and a not-I. But which comes first? The idealist sacrifices the independence of the thing for the independence and freedom of the self. The materialist, conversely, sacrifices the independence of the self. Fichte, however, is uncompromising. Intelligence for him is active, primary. The self is free, ethical, and inter-subjective by definition, and leads finally to Novalis' great intuition "I = You." In other words, the I is ethical by nature. But when the object is taken as fundamental, as it is by the materialist, mind is reduced to an epiphenomenon and the subject loses all moral responsibility and efficacy. Thus Fichte's primary concern is with the morally free, active self. Without this freedom there can be no true ethics. Thus he concludes that to found a practical philosophy we must realize the existence of a higher self or transcendental "I," which is the source of both the lower self or empirical I and the world. In other words, the first task, then, is to realize the activity of the transcendent self as the active principle in consciousness. This cannot be demonstrated logically or conceptually, it can only be done—that is, experienced as the very experience of knowing itself. It cannot be objectified, for it is pure activity or self-enactment, in which there is no longer any foreign element to create a difference between enactment and accomplishment. For Fichte, therefore, all free activity must derive from, and be ascribed to, the transcendent self, the I of one's I.

Besides Fichte and the other philosophers—as well as Goethe and Schiller, each of whom presented in his own way the potential of moving from pure idealism toward a more non-dualistic approach to spirit and matter—Rudolf Steiner, of course, experienced many other, perhaps equally significant, actual human encounters: with teachers, priests, doctors, and many, many others. Given the intensity of his inner life, it is difficult to grasp the extent and complexity of Rudolf Steiner's social life. He loved people. He was passionately interested in them in and for themselves, their individualities. Thus his social life was extraordinarily rich and filled with friendships, some of which lasted throughout his lifetime. Indeed, he needed and always sought a community of friends. One thinks, for instance, of the Spechts, in whose family he lived and whose children he educated; of Rosa Mayreder and Marie Eugenie delle Grazie, whose intellectual salons he frequented; of the Cistercian Wilhelm Neumann, with whom he discussed the nature of Christ; of the poet Fritz Lemmermayer; of his "fatherly friend," the great Goetheanist Karl Julius Schröer, who brought him the task of editing Goethe's scientific writings; of the esotericist and music critic Friedrich Eckstein, who had met Madame Blavatsky and first talked to him of Theosophy. All these and more were truly life teachers, initiators, each of whom contributed in his or her own very human way to Rudolf Steiner's soul development, and whom he was still able to recall with true gratitude and in vivid detail fifty years later in his *Autobiography*.

All such experiences—and above all, many painful and transformative life experiences of inner struggle and outer failure, as well as a passionate ongoing and deep concern for social and political questions—were preparatory to the experience of true meditation and set him on the path to becoming the conscious spiritual researcher we know as Rudolf Steiner. All too often we think of Rudolf Steiner springing "ready-made" from his mother's womb with all his initiate's capacities, as if inherited from past incarnations, requiring only, as it were, to be unwrapped before being able to be put to use. In fact, Rudolf Steiner had to work very hard and suffer deeply before being able to become the spiritual master and teacher we know. In this sense, he was "self-made," as we must all be.

The lesson here perhaps is that if we, each in our own way, would walk in Rudolf Steiner's footsteps—making them our own, as in some sense Anthroposophy asks us to do—we must learn to relate this trajectory not as something foreign to our own lives but intimately, as a living propaedeutic to following the meditative path that he teaches. Each of us must find his or her own unique, individual way of doing this, which may outwardly not appear similar at all.

*

As for Rudolf Steiner's actual path to meditation, perhaps the earliest document that we have from his hand, a letter written when he was nineteen (January 13, 1881), makes evident that the power of his passion to know himself and the world had made him already at the age of nineteen, if not a meditator in any formal sense, at least a meditative thinker of sorts, one almost in a fury to read everything not for information but for anything that might contain a clue to the authentic experience of the reality of the self and world:

> It was the night from January 10th to the 11th. I didn't sleep a wink. I was busy with philosophical problems until about 12:30 a.m. Then, finally, I threw myself down on my couch. All my striving during the previous year had been to research whether the following statement by Schelling was true or not: "Within everyone dwells a secret, marvelous capacity to draw back from the stream of time—out of

> the self clothed in all that comes to us from outside—into our innermost being and there, in the immutable form of the Eternal, to look into ourselves." I believe, and am still quite certain of it, that I have discovered this capacity in myself.... (Rudolf Steiner, Letters, *Briefe*, [German only])

In other words, in some fashion of his own making, he took the sentence from Schelling as a meditative sentence and worked with it intensely and with focused attention until it finally yielded its experience—clearly one related to the I. As for his passion to know, in another letter, six months later (July 27, 1881), explaining why perhaps he was not a perfect correspondent, he writes:

> I am not one of those who dive into the day like an animal in human form. I pursue a quite specific goal, an idealistic aim—knowledge of the truth! This cannot be done offhandedly. It requires the greatest striving in the world, free of all egotism, and equally of all resignation. (Rudolf Steiner, Letters, *Briefe*, [German only])

In his twenties, then, though his breakthroughs (and his selflessness in pursuit of the truth) were remarkable, he was still on the way. He continued to wrestle—proto-meditatively—with "philosophical" issues of space and time, and with the nature of light and color, as well as with beauty as Schiller spoke of it. Positively, what motivated him, on the one hand, was the need to understand the living relation between the invisible, discarnate reality of spirit as he knew it from experience and the visible, incarnate reality of the sensory world; and, on the other, the need to fully experience and hence begin to articulate his intuition or conviction of the transcendental, immortal reality of the I (outside of time) as the transformative source of freedom and love in the world's becoming. Negatively, what impelled him was the self-evident evolutionary need to find an adequate way to dismantle and oppose the pervasive materialism that he could see infecting every aspect of human life and culture.

That this was as much a spiritual as a philosophical path, that the two were already one for him, is made clear in the following extraordinary document, found on two loose note pages, entitled *Credo (or the Individual and the All).* It is dated 1886 (or 1888)—Rudolf Steiner was in his mid-twenties at the time. Though esoteric, its message is clear: the task is to overcome egotism/selfness that separates us from and sets us in opposition over against the world and other human beings. If we do so, if we learn to will "in the Spirit," the central "Light of the Universe" will resurrect in us and we will become full, creative participants in the ongoing, evolving life of creation. The seed of yearning for this reality is planted in all human beings, and Rudolf Steiner describes four spheres or paths through which we can work: knowledge, art, religion, and love. Of these, perhaps surprisingly echoing St. Paul, he seems to suggest that love is the highest.

> The *World of Ideas* is the original source and the principle of all being and existence. Unending harmony and blessed peace are contained in it. Being, not illuminated by its light, would be something dead and lifeless. It would play no part in the life of the world whole. Only what derives its existence from the *Idea* means something on the tree of universal creation. The Idea is Spirit—clear and sufficient *in* itself *with* itself. Whatever is singular, individual, and particular must have the spirit within itself, otherwise it will fall off, go to waste like a dry leaf from the tree, and would have existed in vain.
>
> Human beings feel and know themselves as singular only when they awake to full consciousness. For this reason, yearning for the idea is implanted in them. This yearning leads us to overcome our separateness, or individuality, and allows the Spirit to arise within us and become conformed to the Spirit. We must rise up and cast off everything in us that is selfish, all that defines us as this individual being. For this particularity is what darkens the Light of the Spirit. Everything we do out of sensuality, instinct, desire, or passion only serves the egotistic individuality. We must kill this self-seeking will in us. Instead, as singular beings we must want what the Spirit, the Idea wants in us. Let our singularity move there, and follow the voice of the idea within, because only the Idea is the divine! To will as a separate being is to be a worthless point at the periphery of the universe.

It is to disappear into the stream of time. To will "in the Spirit" is to be at the center, for the central Light of the Universe resurrects in you. If you act as a separate being you lock yourself out of the closed chain of world action. The killing of all selfishness ("selfness") is the foundation for a higher life. Whoever destroys selfness lives in eternal being. To the extent that we have allowed selfness to die within us, we are immortal. Selfness is what is mortal in us. Such is the true meaning of the saying: "If you do not die before you die, when you die, you rot." Those who do not kill the selfishness within them during their lives have no part in the universal life, which is immortal. Such people have never been, and have no true being.

There are four spheres of human activity in which, by killing off all separateness in our lives, we can dedicate ourselves to the spirit. These are the spheres of knowledge (insight), art, religion and the loving devotion in the spirit to a personality. Whoever does not live within one of these four spheres does not live at all. *Knowledge* is dedication to the universal in mind or thought; *art* is dedication to the universal in contemplation; *religion* is dedication to the universal in heart and soul; and *love* is dedication to the universal with all our spiritual forces to what appears to us as a precious being of inestimable value within the totality of all there is. Knowledge is the most spiritual form of selfless dedication. Love is the most beautiful. For love is a truly heavenly light in everyday life. Pious, devout, true spiritual love ennobles our being right down to its innermost fiber. It uplifts all that lives within us. Pure, pious love transforms our whole soul life into another, one that is in relationship with the Spirit of the World. In this highest sense, to love means to bear the breath of divine life to where the most shameful egotism and the most careless passions can be found. Only one who knows something of the holiness of love may speak of true devoutness or piety.

Those who have passed out of separateness and lived through one of the four spheres and into the divine life of the Idea have achieved the goal for which the seed of yearning was placed in their hearts—that is, union with the spirit—which is one's true *destination*. Those who live in the spirit live free. They have disengaged themselves from all secondary things. Nothing can compel them, other than what

> they want to be freely compelled by, for they have known it as the highest.
>
> Let the truth come to life. Lose yourself to find yourself again in the world spirit!

Out of the aspirations, struggles, and frustrations—at once spiritual, psychological, philosophical, and existential—of this period, as well as ongoing and serious engagement with the social issues of the moment, was born *The Philosophy of Freedom.*

First conceived almost a full decade before its completion and springing from his deepest I-experiences, *The Philosophy of Freedom* is not so much a book of philosophy as it is of non-philosophy. Writing to Rosa Mayreder, after invoking Nietzsche and regretting that he was no longer able to read him, Steiner says: "He (Nietzsche) would have seen it for just what it is: personal experience in every single sentence."

> My reason for writing it as I did...was purely subjective. I was not setting forth a doctrine, but simply recording inner experiences through which I had actually passed. And I reported them just as I experienced them. Everything in the book is written from this personal angle, even to the shaping of the thoughts that it contains... My purpose was to write a biographical account of how one human soul made the difficult ascent to freedom... I found my own way up as best I could and then, later on, described the route I had taken. Afterwards, I could have discovered a hundred other different routes...Perhaps the time for handing over theory in a matter like this is already over. Philosophy, except when it is real individual experience holds scarcely any further interest for me. (Rudolf Steiner, Letters [*Briefe*, German only])

No theory, then; and the sanctity of individual experience. This is the lesson—or the beginning of the lesson. For beyond its phenomenological, experiential description of overcoming the dualism of representational "dead" thinking by intuitive "living" thinking—experienced as the link between sensory, conceptual, and spiritual reality—the culmination of his book lays down the intimate, foundational connection of such thinking with morality or ethics (moral imagination). The I is certainly free, but its freedom can manifest only as love. This is perhaps the hallmark of accomplished meditation, for true living thinking is also love. As he writes in the 1918 Addendum to Chapter 8, echoing the *Credo*:

> Whoever truly manages to experience life within thinking sees that dwelling in mere feeling or contemplating the element of will cannot even be compared to (let alone be ranked above) the inner richness and the experience, the inner calmness and mobility in the life of thinking. It is precisely the richness, the inner fullness of experience that makes its reflection in normal consciousness seem dead and abstract... Yet this is only the sharply contoured shadow of the reality of thinking—a reality interwoven with light, dipping down warmly into the phenomena of the world. This dipping down occurs with a power that flows forth from the activity of thinking itself—the power of love in spiritual form.

And not just thinking: "Only when I follow my love for an object is it I myself who act...I acknowledge no outer principle because I have found within myself the basis of my action—love of the action. I do not check rationally whether the action is good or evil: I do it because I love it. My action becomes good if my intuition, steeped in love, stands in the right way in the intuitively experienced world continuum...." In other words: "To live in love of action, to let live in the understanding of the other's will, is the fundamental maxim of free human beings." Again, as he repeatedly emphasizes in his later teaching: "Three steps forward in moral development, for one step forward in knowledge."

Meanwhile, his work editing Goethe's scientific writings—living with Goethe's spirit, in the Goethe Archive, handling papers and objects Goethe himself had handled—deepened and rendered more pragmatic and empirical the insights that he had already gained, enabling him to begin to see the possibility of a "higher," more strictly meditative phenomenology. At the same time, strife—profound disagreements with his editor—and his failure to gain a university position made his personal life, above all his sense of isolation, very difficult. At this point in his unfolding, though he recognized the progress he had made, he nevertheless felt unable to move in his thinking or meditating beyond a kind of conceptual idealism. He had come far, but it seemed he was stuck. This too was a lesson. In fact, it was not until he was about thirty-six, at the end of his time in Weimar, with these earlier trials behind him, that "a profound transformation" took place in his soul, one that became the "decisive experience" around which his meditative life could finally cohere.

The turn began with his discovery of the sense world. The spiritual world had always been self-evident to him, but the sense world had eluded him. This now changed. A new capacity of dedicated attentiveness to sensory-perceptible phenomena awakened, which led to the realization—the experience—that the sense world could reveal something only *it* could it reveal. With this, a new world opened. As he put it in his *Autobiography*: "When the sensory realm is approached objectively, free of all subjectivity, it reveals something about which spiritual insight has nothing to say." At the same time, this experience also made clear the "distinct nature of the spiritual, free of any physical impression."

This distinction between "spiritual" and "physical," however, was not one of fixed opposition. What it made clear was the true mystery of *life*, which demands continuously living within such differences. The task was to remain fully within them. This led to what he called a deep need to "experience life's mysteries," and not just seek to grasp them theoretically, which in turn led to the realization that "a mystery arises within the real world as a phenomenon; the solution arises equally in the reality. Something arises as being or process and solves the problem." The whole world, except for the human being, is a mystery—the actual "world mystery." "Human beings are themselves the solution… Human beings, at any moment, can speak of that universal mystery, but they can never say more of the answer than they have learned about themselves as human beings." Thus he understood how "cognition also becomes a process in reality."

> Questions reveal themselves in the world: answers reveal themselves as realities; knowledge is human participation in what is revealed by the beings and processes of the spiritual and physical worlds…

> This soul experience, with all its intensity at the time, arose from an objective devotion to pure, clear sensory observation ... (This, and the following quotations are from the *Autobiography*)

In other words: "Whenever the substantiality of the sensory world is perceived—not thought—an enigma arises in reality, and the answer to that mystery is in the human being." Succinctly stated:

> As human beings, we are not the beings who create the essence of knowledge for ourselves; rather our soul provides the stage on which the world begins in part to experience its own becoming and existence. Without knowledge the world would remain incomplete.

As a consequence, he writes:

> I increasingly found it possible to defend the nature of human knowledge against the view that human beings merely produce a kind of "copy" of the world in the mind through cognition. In my view of cognition, the human being is a co-creator, not a copier of the world...

In this way, inner experience, as Rudolf Steiner tells it, led him to discover the true nature of meditation as an "absolute necessity for the life of the soul." He was already familiar with two ways of knowing:

> The first is conceptual knowledge gained through sensory observation. Such knowledge is assimilated and then retained according to the power of memory...The second kind of knowledge does not acquire concepts through sensory observation; they are experienced inwardly and free of the senses. The very nature of this experience assures that such concepts are based on spiritual reality. One experiences the fact that concepts contain an assurance of spiritual reality with the same certainty (through the nature of the experience itself) that one has in recognizing the difference between physical reality and illusion when acquiring knowledge of the sensory world.

This second way constituted the meditative path that Rudolf Steiner had come to and practiced up to this point. He stresses that such "ideal spiritual" knowledge cannot be possessed as a memory (unlike the first way of knowing) and was therefore not repeatable, but had to be experienced—assimilated—anew each time. It was an "ongoing process of continual reciprocation with the world thus entered and...occurs through meditation, which...is pursued out of the ideal insight of its value." He adds:

> I had sought this reciprocal relationship long before the transformation in my soul (in my thirty-fifth year). Then it happened that meditation became an absolute necessity for the life of the soul. And along with this, the third kind of knowledge appeared before my inner being.

This third way "led not only deeply into the spiritual world, but allowed a living, intimate union with that world." By "inner necessity," Rudolf Steiner found himself repeatedly having to place at the center of his consciousness "a particular kind of mental image," one not derived from the sense world and with which he was inevitably in the position of an observer, but a "spiritual image" into which, through intense, focused, selfless attention, he could wholly enter and with which he could unite: become one. In other words, this third path—true meditation—is unitive: spiritual reality is directly apprehended without mediation. This is because "in such meditation, practiced out of inner necessity for spiritual life, one becomes increasingly aware of an 'inner human spirit' that can live, perceive, and move within the spiritual realm, entirely detached from the physical organism." Conceptuality recedes. Its place is taken by an element of will. And at the same time, the experience is not bounded, but limitless: the unknown can become known unendingly. One's meditative journey knows no limits. One can grow into every kind of existence. "The 'primordial ground' of existence lies within the totality of human experience..."

Such, then, was the unfolding of Rudolf Steiner's path of meditation, which now became an inner necessity for him as he prepared to leave Weimar and move to Berlin. It was also, we may surmise, what led him, around the turn of the century, in Berlin, to the culminating experience—"decisive for my soul's development"—of the first half of his life. Namely, when, after deep meditative struggles, as he sought to penetrate for himself once and for all the meaning of Christianity, a task that had waited restlessly in his soul until this moment, he found himself finally standing, as he put it, "spiritually before the Mystery of Golgotha in a deep and solemn celebration of knowledge."

What Rudolf Steiner experienced we shall never know exactly. It was his experience. But we can learn from it, each in our own way. In some form he encountered—and was able to cognize consciously—the reality of the being of Christ and his deed. Something happened within the context of deep meditative work and struggle that was perhaps akin to Jacob Boehme's experience polishing his pewter cup when the entire structure and process of the universe, creation, and redemption passed before him in an instant; it then took the rest of his life to work it out. Something similar must have happened to Rudolf Steiner. For Steiner, from this point on, the Mystery of Golgotha became the hidden key to all, determining the rest of his life. Out of it would gradually emerge his master concept or paradigm—the Sacrifice of Golgotha: the Sacrifice of Creation. Unpack this and what you have, roughly stated, is, as we see in *Esoteric Science*, a threefold of metamorphosing sacrificial Love, of free selfless giving, of the highest moral striving, in which the gods, human beings, and the Earth are called to be interwoven in a single path of Love and Sacrifice—a path of sacrificial love or free selfless giving that we are all called to incarnate in our own lives through love of the Earth, love of the gods, and love of one another. With this unique, deeply reverential, awe-inspiring, initiatory experience, Rudolf Steiner was ready to enter onto the world stage. He was prepared. He needed only a vessel, which in due course the Theosophical Society provided.

Sometime in mid-September 1900, Count Brockdorff (1884-1921) asked Rudolf Steiner to give a lecture in the Theosophical Library in Berlin. He did so on September 22. Nietzsche was his topic. As he spoke, he noticed that among those present were some who showed true interest in the spiritual world—an unusual experience for him. Recognizing in the interest a gift not to be refused, and even perhaps a call to speak, Steiner suggested that he return to give a second lecture the following week on "Goethe's Secret Revelation." This, too, was new: "It was an important experience to be able to speak with words created directly from the spiritual world. Until then...circumstances had limited me to hints about the spiritual, allowing it only to be illuminated through my presentations."

Invited to lecture regularly, he accepted, with the proviso, which he would reiterate over and over again as he progressed ever deeper into the Theosophical Movement, that he could and would speak only of experiences gained through his own research. On October 6, therefore, he began a series of twenty-six lectures on medieval mysticism. The following year, the lectures would appear in book form as *Mystics after Modernism.*

Toward the end the year, a Russian woman, Marie von Sivers, who would become his co-worker (and, later, wife), began to attend the lectures. It was a moment of destiny. They met, and the die was cast. She immediately recognized Rudolf Steiner's mission and dedicated herself to it and to him, working tirelessly to help establish and organize his life-path as teacher and initiator of our time. The beginning would not take long. From Steiner's initial entry into Theosophical circles in 1900 and his subsequent decision to link his own work with Theosophy, it would take only two years for a German Section of the Theosophical Society to be founded in October 1902 with Rudolf Steiner as its general secretary, leader and teacher.

From the beginning, Rudolf Steiner gave the highest priority to the building up of "a core of meditators": "I will build upon the power that makes it possible for me to bring spiritual students onto the path of development. That alone is what assuming this function must mean."

In July 1903, nine months later, the entries in *Mantric Sayings* begin. As they progress, we may trace how they gradually unfold a narrative, find their way, develop a vocabulary, a way of writing/speaking and lay down a path of experience—in the first place, Rudolf Steiner's own experience, and secondly, often the experience of the person they were first entrusted to, and finally—and perhaps most significantly, since they are now offered to us as mediations we, too, could do—the possibility of our own experience. At the same time, the chronological range from 1903 to 1924 makes it possible to correlate the entries to the metamorphosing sequence of lecture courses and different key events in the unfolding of Anthroposophy, as well as, for instance, the three volumes of the Esoteric Lessons. But, in a sense, this is secondary. However instructive and useful such a study might be for a deeper understanding of the "soul" of the teaching, the primary usefulness of this collection is to provide us with potential content for meditation. From this point of view, perhaps the best way to approach the collection is to read into it for a while, and then select a particular meditation that calls you, and meditate it. If even only one meditation calls you, and you make it part of your daily life, the book has served its purpose.

For those unfamiliar with meditation, *How to Know Higher Worlds* and the relevant chapters of *Theosophy* and *Esoteric Science, an Outline* should be consulted, as well as the introductory volume of lectures, *First Steps in Inner Development*. These and works such as *From the History and Contents of the First Section of the Esoteric School* and *Guidance in Esoteric Training*, for instance, contain, for those who are interested, the context within which these meditations were received and given. For a more general overview, the anthology *Start Now* gives a good overview of the many kinds of meditation and practice that Rudolf Steiner made available for his students over the years of his teaching. Very important, too, are the larger "life rules" that he repeatedly stressed—above all, the golden rule of three steps in the perfection of one's character toward the good, for one step forward in knowledge.

In other words, one must never forget the practice on the anthroposophical spiritual path of the essential soul dispositions conducive to practical ethics and a fully realized human life—chief among these being the cultivation of such virtues as reverence, dedication, wonder, humility, perseverance, patience, rhythm in one's life, and interest in and love for life itself and other human beings and the world. Put another way, this is a heart-centered path.

More radiant than the Sun,
Purer than the snow,
Finer than the ether,
Is the Self,
The Spirit in my heart.
This Self am I.
I am this Self.

As Steiner puts it in the second volume of the Esoteric Lessons:

> An occult saying states: "All paths into the spiritual world go through the heart." During meditation we can feel how from every point of our external physical body lines go toward a center point. This middle point is the heart. In their further course these lines continue on in the opposite direction into the spiritual world. This is like a feeling of Christ within us.

In this volume, as a brief meditation for Lucie Bürgi, c. 1912-1913:

> The meaning of the world lies in the heart of human beings.

Clearly, Rudolf Steiner's invocation of the centrality of the heart has many different and esoteric levels and dimensions of meaning. And certainly, the heart is no metaphor. In a sense, it should be taken literally. Perhaps the simplest and most relevant indication in this context is that to place one's consciousness in the heart—to be oriented in one's meditation and one's life toward the heart—is to be open toward the other, toward the future. It is where the aspiration for the union of love and knowledge may be fulfilled. This is also true of the verses and sentences in this book. Received from the spiritual world, by their form, rhythm, and language, they are likewise turned wholly toward it. They create an open space, a site, for heart-oriented practice in the same direction: toward the other, the future, for the sake of the world. However, in a sense, all this is beside the point. One can—and perhaps it is best to—enter into this book directly, with no more preparation than an open heart and an open mind. The meditations themselves will work their magic and teach us.

Thus, opening appropriately with notebook entries explicitly entitled "Meditation," the first entry gives us the reason why we meditate: our self should mean more to the world tomorrow—after our meditation—than it does today. In other words, we meditate to become a new person, different today than yesterday, not for our own selves but for the sake of the world. If, however, we fail to meditate, the second notebook entry tells us, this is not simply a mistake, but in fact a neglect of duty. It is our duty to work out of the spirit. "To work out of the spirit" for the sake of the world thus becomes a definition or description of meditation. The third entry gives yet another definition: to meditate is to become a stage where the eternal and the transitory meet, so that our actions can become those of the eternal, of which we are but mediators; we are the eyes and hands of the primal spirit, which sees and creates through us. Out of the spirit, then, let us create a better world.

In two meditations dedicated to Clara Motzkus (an early Theosophical Society member and painter in whose house meetings were held) — one dense and obscure, the other, a meditation in two sequences on "Aum" is pure and clear. Rather than the holy Hindu triad of "Being, Consciousness, and Bliss" (*Satchitananda*), Rudolf Steiner speaks of "Wisdom, Love, and Being" in two sequences that echo each other, but with significant differences, requiring meditation in themselves. Thus, with careful reading and much pondering and meditative thinking an initially apparently straightforward meditation can become quite challenging. This, too, is part of the process. Indeed, it is what makes later meditation into a process. Simply reading through the mantric sayings, therefore, and thinking about each one, can itself be a kind of meditation and preparation for meditation.

The entries thereafter unfold seamlessly, requiring us to pay attention to nuances, subtle differences, for though the same meditation is never repeated, some seem the same, when actually they are not. Some early sayings are more aphoristic:

> Love's truth lies in love;
> Seek love's root in truth—
> So speaks your higher self.

> The fire's glow turns wood into a warming ray,
> Knowing's resolving will turns work into force.

> Let your work be the shadow that your I casts when it is shone upon by the flame of your higher self.

> Without faith, work remains dead:

Faith stokes the breath of the work, and bears it into the heights of the ether,
it draws the breath of the work into itself and brings it as a sacrifice of becoming to being.

Notebook, July 1903

A thought can be only an orientation,
But the orientation is a stream of light;
and light is the leader of life
in every moment.

For Maria v. Strauch-Spettini, March 1904

Others speak to the fundamental soul quality of inner peace, stillness—the *sine qua non* of meditation. We find such mantric sayings virtually throughout. As Rudolf Steiner writes in *First Steps in Inner Development*: "Inner training takes place in complete inner peace, silently…" In other words: "create moments of inner peace for yourself…" "Practice spirit beholding in stillness of thought…" "In stillness the soul finds its way…" For instance:

You rest in the divine world
You sense yourself in divine peace
Your soul experiences divine peace
Divine peace streams in you.

For Moriz Piza, c. 1906

In YOU, YOU spirit of the world
I myself will find myself
Find that the stillness of YOUR being
Will bring me peace of soul
Peace that leads me
In the paths of life and goals of life:
  I in YOU.

For Auguste Daeglau, c. 1910-1911

I find myself in myself
Divine power grasps me
In the radius of my being
I grasp divine power
In the middle of my heart
Thus I find my spirit
Giving
Peace, peace, peace
To my soul yearning for God.

For Friedrich Wilhelm von Flotow, 1924

As the volume progresses, they become deeper, more complex, more esoteric. For instance:

From cosmic depths
Filled with riddles
Matter's rich fullness
Presses on the human mind
It streams in soul depths
From cosmic heights
Filled with content
By the clarifying light of the spirit
They find their way in human beings
To wisdom-filled reality.

For Lina Schliephak-Utter, December 5, 1910

Cube of salt
The form dissolving in water
The color becoming living
And unfolding into a lily
Out of it a white butterfly soaring up
Into a thinking spirit-being
Flying into the universe

Notebook, c. 1911

Spirit: It thinks me: Piety
Christ: It weaves me: Gratitude
Father: It acts me: Devotion.

For Julius Breitenstein, December 22, 1912

Ahriman, you are the cold spirit
You carry my soul off
Into the realm of hostility to humankind —

Lucifer, you are the force of fire
You carry my soul off
Into the sphere of self-will's power.

I must go between the two —
Through the Christ's binding power in the world
Through Christ's sacrificing power of work.

Notebook, November 1920

Sayings of this kind, however, represent only a fraction of the treasure contained in this volume. Sections follow on "meditations for the days of the week," "for strengthening life forces," and "to provide help for others." These are followed by wartime meditations, meditations for the dead, and memorial verses. All these are surprisingly contemporary and speak to our hearts' needs today. May they bring succor to all who work with them!

Bibliography and Some Related Works by Rudolf Steiner

Autobiography (CW 28)
First Steps in Inner Development
Learning to See into the Spiritual World
How to Know Higher Worlds (CW 10)
Theosophy (CW 9)
Esoteric Science, an Outline (CW 13)
A Way of Self Knowledge and The Threshold of the Spiritual World (CW 16/17)
Guidance in Esoteric Training
From the History and Contents of the Esoteric School (CW 264)
Esoteric Lessons, Volumes I, II, and III (CW 226 1/2/3)
Soul Exercises: Word and Symbol Meditations (CW 267)
Verses and Meditations
Truth-Wrought-Words

I

Mantric Sayings and Meditations

From writings in notebooks and loose note sheets

In chronological order

SOUL EXERCISES

Höhe des Geistes kann nur erklommen werden,
wenn durch das Tor der Demut geschritten wird.

Dr. Rudolf Steiner

1904

The heights of the spirit can be scaled only by passing through the gate of humility.

Dr. Rudolf Steiner

Meditation

Question: You strive for self-knowledge? When you have achieved such knowledge will your so-called self mean more to the whole of the world tomorrow than it means today?

First answer: No, not if you are no different tomorrow than you are today, and your insight or knowledge tomorrow only repeats your being today.

Second answer: Yes, if you are a different person tomorrow than you are today, and your new being tomorrow is the consequence of the insight you gained today.

July 1903

Meditation

Those who deny the cosmic spirit do not know that they are denying themselves. — Such people, however, do not simply make a mistake; rather, they neglect their primary duty:

to work out of the spirit themselves.

September 1903

We are at a stage on which the eternal and the transitory meet —
our knowing is an experience of the eternal, for which we ourselves are
organs of cognition —
our actions are the actions of the eternal, for which we are only
mediators —

Therefore, understand:

I. You are the eye of the primal spirit —
It sees its creation through you.

II. You are the hand of the primal spirit
It creates its creation through you.

Loose note sheet
c. 1903

Through the power of thinking, you move, treading the surging flood of exceptional being and follow the seven directing forces under the guidance of truth;
Desire pulls you backward, placing the directing forces within the power of unbelief;
Spirit pulls you forward, raising the seven to the sounding Sun.

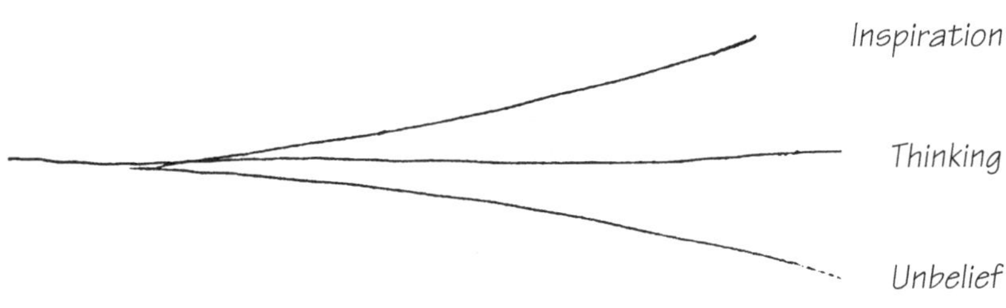

Notebook, 1903

1. In exceptional being, discover the law:
for the law wove the first of the seven into matter.

2. In movement, discover life:
for life poured the second of the seven into matter.

3. In desire, discover the person:
for the person imprinted the third of the seven into matter.

4. In thought, discover yourself:
for the I gave the fourth of the seven its self.

5. In your desire, discover renunciation:
for it was through renunciation that the fifth of the seven sacrificed itself so that you might be a self.

6. In your movement, discover blessed peace:
for the sixth of the seven sacrificed blessed peace, so that, as a living self, you could move yourself.

7. In your exceptional being, discover your eternal law:
for, as eternal law, the seventh of the seven created your self in separation, and as eternal law will lead it out of this state of separation.

For Clara Motzkus
Notebook, 1903

Aum – Unite yourself, O my soul
With the wisdom, which I honor,
And that streams through all,
Whence all comes,
And whither all returns;
I call on this wisdom,
That its light might lead me.

Aum – Unite yourself, O my soul
With universal love, which I honor,
And which streams through all,
Whence all comes,
And whither all returns;
I call on this love,
That its light might lead me.

Aum – Unite yourself, O my soul
With primal being, which I honor,
And which is in all,
Whence all comes,
And whither all returns;
I call on this being,
That its light might lead me.

Aum – Illuminate, O primal being,
My soul, which honors you,
And which comes from you,
And returns to you;
My soul calls upon you,
That it might be led by you.

Aum – Illuminate, O universal love,
My desires, which honor you,
And which come from you,
And return to you;
They shall call on you,
That they might be led by you.

Aum – Illuminate, O wisdom,
My life, so that it lives you,
So that it comes from you,
And returns to you;
Let it call upon you,
That it might be led by you.

For Clara Motzkus
1903

Love's truth lies in love;
Seek love's root in truth —
So speaks your higher self.

The fire's glow turns wood into a warming ray,
Knowing's resolving will turns work into force.

Let your work be the shadow that your I casts when it is shone upon by the flame of your higher self.

Without faith, work remains dead:
Faith stokes the breath of the work, and bears it
into the heights of the ether,
it draws the breath of the work into itself and brings it
as a sacrifice of becoming to being.

July 1903
Notebook

Understand: that you stand on your feet.
Understand: that you work in the earthly realm.
Understand: that you act with human force.

Understand: that you live by the nearness of the Sun.
Understand: that your work in the solar system exhausts itself.
Understand: that your life within humanity exhausts itself.

Understand: that you sense what the elements can give to you.
Understand: that you want what the elements can place in you.
Understand: that you are an elemental spirit that has become human.

Understand: that you should determine yourself through your actions.
Understand: that you should free yourself through your thinking.
Understand: that you should divinize yourself through your meditation.

Notebook
c. 1903-1904

I absorb the stream of being
I stream out of my being into the whole world

I absorb the life of all beings
I stream out of my life to all beings

I absorb the feeling of all that lives
I stream out of my feeling to all that lives.

---

4. I absorb into myself human thinking
   I stream out of meaning-filled will to all people

5. The being-wisdom of all things is woven in me
   I stream out of myself the gift of grace of wisdom

6. The creative power of the world glows within me
   I stream out of myself the power I have received.

7. Eternally living being lives in me
   I live in eternally living being.

For Franz Seiler
1904

A thought can be only an orientation,
But the orientation is a stream of light;
and light is the leader of life
in every moment.

For Maria v. Strauch-Spettini
March 1904

The force of blossoming is called to life by light
The force of desire [or "wishing"] is called to love by the spirit

Notebook
Autumn 1904

I pledge myself to myself:	a
I pledge myself to humanity:	u
I pledge myself to life	m

Loose note sheet
E. S. Berlin, December 21, 1904

Father
Word
Spirit

The Father reveals himself to the Word
The Word reveals himself to the Spirit
The Spirit reveals itself to the Father

The Father hides himself in the Son
and reveals himself to the Spirit
The Son hides in the Spirit
and reveals himself to the Father
The Spirit hides in the Father
and reveals itself to the Son
The Father reveals himself [to himself].

For the lecture, Berlin, July 2, 1904
Notebook

Spirit all around me on all sides
I = a wave in undulating cosmic spirit.
The spirit streams into the I
The spirit streams out of the I
I want to grasp the spirit
I want to protect the spirit
In the spirit-I, universal spirit experiences universal spirit.

Notebook, 1904

I draw in the spirit
I calm the movement
I encompass the spirit

I burn as spirit
I illuminate as spirit
I name spirit

I am spirit.

Notebook, 1904

I sacrifice sensation – green
I sacrifice desire – indigo
I sacrifice myself – yellow

I want thought – red
I want love – orange
I want being – violet

Notebook, 1904

Filled with devotion, my heart senses
The lofty spirit
That radiates through all space;
Sensing it, my soul's deepest inner life
Comes to know it.
It will illuminate and warm me,
If, striving and thinking, I always seek to approach it.

For Helene Lehmann
c. 1905-1906

Immediately upon waking:
Remain unresponsive to sensory impressions.
Think nothing else but:

Self in spirit
You preside in the realm of the spheres
You shine in light
You work in fire
You are wisdom, beauty, and strength
You are I
I will be you.

For Johanna Mücke
c. 1906

In pure beams of light
Shines the divinity of the world.
In the pure fire of the ether
Beams the high power of selfhood.
I rest in the spirit of the world,
I will always find myself
In the eternal spirit of the world.

Strength in my soul

For Johanna Mücke
c. 1906

I wish to rest in the divinity of the world
To find myself in the divinity of the world
To find myself and rest at peace within myself
At peace surrendering myself to God's mercy
Feeling the grace of the spirit powers within me
Feeling blessed peace through them
Calling on them for my soul.

For Margarete v. Ploetz
c. 1906

You rest in the divine world
You sense yourself in divine peace
Your soul experiences divine peace
Divine peace streams in you.

For Moriz Piza
c. 1906

I rest in the divinity of the world
I live in the soul of the world
I think in the spirit of the world.

c. 1906
Notebook

Spirits from below: retain what is evil
Spirits from above: give what is good
Hover around, spirits of the universe,
Sacrificing to the One radiating all around.

Notebook, 1906

I extol all-presiding harmony
In the house of the worlds
I thank the fire spirits for the wisdom of numbers
I praise souls of love for the goodness of measure
I feel the stability of the building in the bearing forces
Thus thanking, praising, feeling
I grasp God's creative tones echoing within me.

For Hans Blieffert
Beginning of February 1906

Three pairs resolve the riddle of being:
Force and number, light and wisdom,
Warmth and desire; their binding and loosening
Unlocks the "great world" for the researcher;
And if their uniting and dividing
Can reveal themselves in his soul
He stands in the spiritual realm.

Draft

If I require force
I will research the secret of numbers
If I yearn for wisdom
I will seek being in the light
If I strive for revelation
It will grow in me in the warmth of life.

Draft

May the goal of my research be
How force and number
How light and wisdom
How warmth and desire
Are found in the universe

Draft

Three pairs of eternal being and life
Unveil to me
The riddle of the great
And the small world:
Force and number
Light and wisdom
Warmth and will

Force and number
Light and wisdom
Warmth and will
You three pairs
Of eternal being and of life
Unveil to me
The riddle of both the outside
And the inside of the world.

Notebook, 1906

Deeds and words discourse
Feeling and thought speak
Thus the world veils its essence
Learn to be silent and you will become

—

Learn to be silent and your spirit will become powerful
Give yourself to the power

—

I want to see the power of the spirit
By practicing silence
I will enter the realm of the spirit
By wanting to
The spirit's wanting should become mine
Through feeling

—

If I learn to be silent in deeds and words
I will be able to grasp the spirit forcefully

Draft fragments

Learn to be silent and power will come to you.
Give yourself to the power and wanting-desire will come to you.
Give yourself to the wanting and feeling will come to you.
Give yourself to feeling and insight will come to you.

E.S. Cologne, December 1, 1906

The human I creates riddles
Riddles in the Sun's light
Riddles in the dark night
But the light that solves every riddle
Shines in the true spirit
Unites the heart to this spirit
The peace of wisdom radiates to me.

Notebook, 1907

Steadfastly I place myself into existence,
I let myself be led by the force of the spirit,
I wish to rest in God's essence,
I wish to seek myself in spirit-being.
I will find myself in myself
When I find God in the universe.
Thus I will live forever and ever.

For Wilhelm Gneiting-Zimmermann
c. 1907

1. In the pure beams of light
2. Divinity illuminates the world
3. In the depths of my own being
4. Emanates the divinity of my self
5. I live in the divinity of the world
6. I find myself always in the divinity of the world
7. I find my self there.

For Henry B. Monges
c. 1907

In pure beams of light
The spirit of the world shines
In pure warmth for all beings
The soul of a life shines
I rest in the soul of the world
I will find myself
In the spirit of the world.

Notebook, 1908

1.

In the darkness I find the existence of God

2.

In rose-red I feel the source of all life

3.

In ether-blue the spirit's yearning rests

4.

In the green of life the breath of all life breathes

5

In golden yellow the clarity of thought shines

6

In fire-red the strength of the will is rooted

7

In Sun-white the kernel of my being reveals itself.

Draft
Notebook, 1908

In the morning:

> In me is an I that works from far to close and
> from close to far.

Darkness:	In darkness still find divine being.
Rose-red:	In rose-red I feel the source of all life.
Blue:	In ether-blue the soul finds itself in devotion.
Green:	In green of life the breath of all life breathes.
Yellow:	In golden yellow clarity of thought shines.
Red:	In the red of fire the strength of the will is forged.
White:	In Sun-white the kernel of my being reveals itself.

Loose note sheet
1908

The I is all beings
All beings are the I

The I receives the revelation of beings
The revelation of beings radiates from the I

The I has the activity of beings in itself
The I overcomes activity of the beings

The I is born of the activity that is overcome
The activity that is overcome detaches itself from the I.

Notebook, 1908

Evenings: Truths from Theosophy

Mornings: After the ⊕ and after recalling truths from Theosophy:

I rest in the divinity of the world
I want to live in the soul of the world
I want to think in the spirit of the world.

For Marie Kaiser
c. 1908

Meditation for protection from without

My aura's outer sheath condenses.
May it surround me with an impenetrable vessel
Against all impure, corrupt thoughts and sensations.
May it open itself only to divine wisdom.

For Elsa Möller
and E. S. Kassel, February 26, 1909

From light-giving Sun
Through life-giving streaming
Into the receiving human soul
To the supporting Earth —

Notebook, 1910

In the pure beams of light
We find rest and strength
In the pure warmth of souls
We find strength and rest
You will find yourself
In the world's divinity
Now and always.

For Otto and Anna Rebmann
1910

In YOU, YOU spirit of the world
I myself will find myself
Find that the stillness of YOUR being
Will bring me peace of soul
Peace that leads me
In the paths of life and goals of life:
        I in YOU.

For Auguste Daeglau
c. 1910-1911

The spirit's being fills
The expanses of space
Animates the sequence of the ages
Shapes for sensation
The animal's soul-bodily nature
And in human beings
Tears itself from outer work
To see itself.

Loose note sheet, 1910

I am a cosmic tone
Sounding in cosmic space.
Living in the tone as world-feeling
Forcefully draws forth from me the word.

For Alma von Brandis
c. 1910

Michael!
Prestami la tua spada
Affinché io sia armato
Per vincere il drago in me.
Empimi della tua forza
Affinché io sgomini
Gli spiriti che vogliono paralizzarmi.
Agisci dunque in me
In modo tale che risplenda la luce
del mio io e possa cosí esser condotto
A quelle azioni degne di te.
Michael!

Michael!
Lend me your sword
That I may be armed
To vanquish the dragon in me.
Fill me with your strength
That I may bring into confusion the spirits
Who wish to paralyze me.
Work in me
So that the light irradiates
My I, and that I may be led
To deeds worthy of you.
Michael!

For Giovanni Colazza
c. 1910

Light's weaving being radiates
Through the vastness of space,
To fill the world with being.
Love's blessing warms
The course of the ages,
To call for the revelation of all worlds.
And messengers of the spirit
Marry light's weaving being
With soul's revelation;
And when the human being marries
Its own self with both,
It lives in the spirit's heights.

Munich, August 1910

Light's weaving being radiates
From person to person,
To fill the world with truth.
Love's blessing warms
Soul upon soul,
To spread blessedness on all worlds.
And spirit messengers marry
Human works of blessing
With world goals;
And if human beings, who find themselves among human beings,
Can unite both, then spirit light will radiate through soul warmth.

Munich, August 1910

In the light-air of spirit-land
The roses of the soul bloom,
And their redness shines
Into the heaviness of the earth;
In the human essence this is condensed
To the image of the heart:
It radiates in the force of the blood
As the rose-red of the earth
And radiates back into the fields of spirit.

For Mieta Waller
c. 1910

⊕

In the divinity of the world
My being rests
In the spirit of the world
My soul rests
In the soul of the world
My spirit rests
Forever and ever.

For Walter Hering
November 21, 1910

God in me supports me and builds me myself
on me through myself.

Wrongs done to me are the appearance
of wrongs within me.

To know myself in myself means
to reveal myself through myself
to myself for myself.

Out of me comes forth only
what I create in myself through myself
in order in myself to reveal myself to myself.

Notebook, 1910

From cosmic depths
Filled with riddles
Matter's rich fullness
Presses on the human mind
It streams in soul depths
From cosmic heights
Filled with content
By the clarifying light of the spirit
They find their way in human beings
To wisdom-filled reality.

For Lina Schliephak-Utter
December 5, 1910

Cosmic thoughts live in your thinking,
Cosmic forces weave in your feeling,
Cosmic beings work in your willing.
Lose yourself in cosmic thoughts,
Experience yourself through cosmic forces,
Create yourself out of will beings.
Do not end with thinking's dream game
In the cosmic distances — ;
Begin in the vastness of the spirit,
And end in your own soul's depths — ;
You will find the goals of the gods:
Knowing yourself in yourself.

Munich, August 1911

Cosmic thoughts live in my thinking
Cosmic powers weave in my feeling
Will beings work in my willing

I want to know myself
In world thoughts
I want to experience myself
In cosmic powers
I want to create myself
In will beings

In this way I do not end at the world's ends
Nor at the vastness of space
I begin at the world's ends
And at the vastness of space
And I end only with myself
Knowing myself in myself.

For a [male] Russian anthroposophist, 1912

Those must sacrifice separate being and life
Who will behold the spirit's goals
Through the senses' revelation;
Who will make bold
To pour the will of the spirit
Into their own will.

Munich, August 1911

May thought interpret for me
May feeling lead me
To the essence of the will

The cosmic ways
To my own place
In the spirit-field

I am.

Notebook, 1911

In the small grain of seed
Tremendous growth conceals itself

What is greatest rests
Soul-natured in this tiny thing

And soul-natured within me
My spirit's being strives
To behold itself in cosmic distances.

Notebook, 1911

May my soul feel deeply cosmic spirit
Glancing spiritually into the universe
My soul recovers its spirit power
Turning itself back within itself
Finding power, itself within itself
To hold
To support.

For Antoinette Fabre
c. 1911

Cube of salt
The form dissolving in water
The color becoming living
And unfolding into a lily
Out of it a white butterfly soaring up
Into a thinking spirit-being
Flying into the universe

Notebook, c. 1911

I look at the plant
I leave the Earth
Two forces preside:
Sunward light-beams
Wound around
By spiraling streams of warmth.
Filled with soul I think to myself
That what streams from such beings
Separates plant-warmth
From plant-light.
If I can quicken plant-light
Into a flame,
That sheds the warmth from itself
As the human sheds its body in death,
This leads me into Devachan.

Notebook, c.1911

I place before me the image of a lion
As he appears to me in form and color
As he grows from small to large
As he races in passionate pursuit
All of this takes place in the physical realm
But this does not exhaust all of the possibilities of his being
From above I allow an
Invisible image of light
To stream down upon him
Ensouled with feelings
Which long for the earthly realm
And led by the will
To earthly creation
Then I let into this structure of light
Streaming upward from below
Longing that strives for the vastness of the worlds
And is held down by an upper structure
Then all that the eye sees should disappear
And what remains will lead me into the astral realm.

Notebook, c. 1911

1. Peace, lead my seeking soul
In its searching for the good

2. Truth, lead my striving soul
In its striving for the light

3. God in me, lead me myself
In all searching
for light, love, knowledge.

For Anna Wager Gunnarsson
April 20, 1912

You, my soul, embolden yourself
To make use of your own forces.

August 1912

Spirit:	It thinks me :	Piety
Christ:	It weaves me :	Gratitude
Father:	It affects me :	Devotion.

For Julius Breitenstein
December 22, 1912

Es denkt mich Frömmigkeit
Es webt mich Dankbarkeit
Es wirkt mich Andacht Ehrerbietung

E. d. n. i. ... m. p. s. s. r.
theos.

It thinks me Piety
It weaves me Gratitude
It acts me Devotion, reverence

E. d. n. *I. ... m.* *P. s. s. r.*
[Ex deo nascimur In Christo morimur Per spiritum sanctum reviviscimus]
[From God we are born in Christ we die through the Holy Spirit we live again]

theos[soph]

For Max Kändler
December 1912

It weaves me: Gratitude
It thinks me: Piety
It acts me: Devotion, Reverence.

For Lucie Bürgi, December 1912

Liebe Weisheit Leben
erfüllet mir
Herz Seele Geist

Любовь, мудрость, жизнь
наполняютъ мнѣ
Сердце, душу, духъ.

Love Wisdom Life
Fill me
Heart Soul Spirit

For a [male] Russian anthroposophist
c. 1912

My soul turns
    itself upward,
    to feel
    the motherly world spirit.

My soul turns
    itself downward,
    to feel
    the fatherly earth soul.

I, your son,
    seek you,
    to receive
    light, love, truth.

For Rudolf Toepell
c. 1912-1913

[English by Rudolf Steiner or the recipient]

God is one.
He manifests himself in three aspects,
If in the world's space
The soul senses the motherly spirit of the spheres,
If out of the depths of the Earth
The soul feels the fatherly soul of life,
Then in the third, in the human being,
One manifests in Three;
Three in One.

For a [male] English anthroposophist
c. 1912-1913

Der Sinn der Welt liegt im Herzen
der Menschen

The meaning of the world lies in the heart
of human beings

For Lucie Bürgi
c. 1912-1913

Extended in the distances of space
Spread out in the being of time
I feel the all-presiding spirit
And if I look into myself
I feel it within me
I feel both as one
I find God within me.

For Walter Hering
January 11, 1913

Ich leuchte
Aus Seelenleib
Seelenleib zehret
Am Sonnenleib
Sonnenleib weset im Sinnenleib
So bin ich
Als zehrende Flamme —
Leben

I glow
From the soul-body
The soul-body lives
Off the Sun-body
The soul-body is in the sense-body
Thus I *am*
As a living flame —
Life

For Lucie Bürgi
c. 1913

Soul-I, on the soul's foundations, you are
in the soul-space within me,
Soul-space, your words work in vast expanses,
Soul-foundations, your forces work in the depths.

For Karl Wendel
1913

In the expanses of the universe
The force bestirred itself
That gave my soul existence
Sensing this I will remember this force
Trustingly hope for it
May it bring me the light
that always lights my life.

For Else Mletzko
1913

If I look up at the Sun
God appears to me in the light
If I feel my own heart
God's force beats in my blood
I will nurture this
As often as my soul urges me
To look upon God's goodness
And I will pray
That my soul will urge me often
Thus I will gain peace
Thus I will gain strength
And true life force.

For Karla-Ruth Holz, 1913

1. God in me
2. Spirit in every world gesture
3. Unmoved mover

For Trifon G. Trapesnikov
c. 1913

Far away the spirit-image beckons
And the spirit-image is with God
And the spirit-image is a god
In it is the living I
And the living I is the light of human beings.

Loose note sheet
probably 1914

In pure will the gods preside
They sow the seeds and make them grow.
In pure will they harvest the fruit,
And no one wants who eats this fruit.

For Ellen Rennit
July 17, 1914

Von oben in Ja
~~Von links in~~
Von vorne in aum
Von links in MEB
So bist du
So lebst du
So sinnest du
In ⊕

From above in Ja
From the front in aum
From the left in M E B
Thus you are
Thus you live
Thus you meditate
In ⊕

Draft, 1914
Notebook

From above Ja
From the front Aum
From the left M E B

Thus you are
Thus you live
Thus you meditate

In ⊕

Stillness in consciousness

Loose note sheet, 1914

Force lives	–	head
My soul	–	heart
In stillness	–	lung
In me	–	entire body
And leads	–	hands
My existence	–	in hovering
In safety	–	guardian spirit

Notebook, 1915

In luminous heights
Where, glistening in the Sun
The friendly dragonflies*
Fluttering rays of warmth
Become one with their habitat
Linger O you my soul:
They weave my remembering
Strength out of sorrow;
Already I feel
How they feel me;
How warming they stream
Penetratingly through me;
The spirit melts
In world weaving
Earth's heaviness
Into future's light.

Draft, Notebook

[*See note on page 342-43]

In luminous heights
Where glistening in the Sun
The friendly *Libillen** are
Moving, streaming warmth
Linger, O you my soul
In thinking
Feel yourself departing!
The force you use
To fly to the heights
Unburdens you
Of the feeling of bodily heaviness.
Now feel too
What you have thought!
The thought-dream is not a dream
When you my soul
In feeling truly live!

Loose note sheet
March 5, 1915

[*See note on page 342-43]

The bright light of the Sun
Streams from the heights
And spirit forces live
In the sunshine's light.
The warmth of the heart
Lives within the human being
And soul forces stream
From the warm chamber of the heart.
In the spirit of the sunlight
God's wisdom presides
In the warm power of the heart
May the soul's love preside.

For Martha Kraul, c. 1915

Darkness permeates the world
It is depicted in the black wood of the cross
Light releases from the darkness
Bright roses streaming sevenfold
Are the revealers of the light
And to you, my soul,
The secret discloses itself.

(Stillness of the soul)

For Arild Rosenkrantz
1915

Prayer

O you powers in the spiritual world,
let me out of my physical body
to be knowing in the world of light,
to be in the light,
to observe my own body of light,
do not allow the power of the ahrimanic forces
to have too much power over me,
so they do not make it impossible for me
to behold what is taking place in my body of light.

Lecture, Dornach, January 2, 1916

The creating spirit of the world
Weaves in the vastness of the world;
Out of the vastness of the world
The force of life streams into my soul.

For Lucie Bürgi
1916

Root-force of my soul
Turn my I toward you
Then the spirit's force streams
Through all my being.

Draft, Notebook

A breath from the spiritual world is what
Streams into the body when awakening
Streams out of the body when falling asleep
As the being of the I experiences itself
In the oscillating meaning of existence

In the breathing of spiritual weaving I am
As air is in the lungs
I am no lung; no, I am a breath of air
Yet what knows of me is lung:
If I grasp this — I know myself
In the spirit of the world. —

For Marie Steiner
March 15, 1916

Seek your I
In the forms of being
In the being of life
In the life of thinking
Think in feeling
Feel in willing
The willing forming
Your I

Your I
Shapes your willing
Your willing is the conscience of your feeling
Your feeling is the conscience of your thinking
Your thinking weaves your life
Your life bears your being
In the shaping of worlds your being moves
Your I toward its goal.

For Karl Habel
c. 1916

Words for meditation to take hold of the will

Victorious spirit
Blaze through the powerlessness
Of faint-hearted souls.
Burn up the I's desires
Kindle compassion,
So that selflessness,
The stream of life for humankind,
Will surge as the source
Of spiritual rebirth.

September 20, 1919

I feel light around me,
It is the light of the world;
I feel light in me,
It is the light of humankind;
And I want to receive
The light of humankind as the light of the world,
The light of the world as the light of humankind.

For Georg-Moritz von Saxony-Altenburg
after 1919

Ahriman, you are the cold spirit
You carry my soul off
Into the realm of hostility to humankind —

Lucifer, you are the force of fire
You carry my soul off
Into the sphere of self-will's power.

I must go between the two —
Through the Christ's binding power in the world
Through Christ's sacrificing power of work.

Notebook, November 1920

In the primal beginning shone the light;
And the light came from the spirit;
And the light was a spirit.
And spirit becomes the light,
When I perceive the light
Through the divine
That works in my soul.

For Otto Wagner, 1919-1923

Für Ferreri =

In mir lebt das Weltensein als Menschenform und Menschengehalt.

Within me lives the existence of the world
As human form and human content.

For Charlotte Ferreri
1920

With resolve should cognizing souls
Penetrate themselves:
With the resolve
To behold the spirit
Who stands at the gate
Reminding us:
To behold in willing
    Beholding to experience
    Experiencing to become
    HIM
    In HIM
    To work
Working in the world's being
    To be
        Really human.

Notebook, 1920

May my soul raise itself
In devotion to the spirit of God
Who lives there in the souls of all the hierarchies
As I live in my thoughts
And I want to feel myself One
With this spirit of God
And feel his power within me.

Loose note sheet
c. 1920

I want to think powerfully
Want to reflect often and powerfully
How within me the spirit's primal force
Inspires me at all times
I want to feel strongly within me
The soul's weaving and the will's power
I want to reflect in stillness
So that in the heart's depths I can find
A foothold when still my soul
Rests in itself and also strong
Wants to act out of itself.

Loose note sheet
c. 1920

Insight speaks to the human soul:
Bear in mind destiny
Behold it patiently;
In beholding it you will become
In enduringly feeling it you will become:
Gain your freedom
In freedom your bond
With another soul's
    Being.

For Edith Maryon
February 9, 1921

Christ, the Sun-Love-Word
Lives in the beam of light
That penetrates my eye.
And may Christ live
In my whole being,
And with my whole being
May I live in Christ.

With great feeling meditate each individual line.

For Johanna de Boer-Gerlach
May 1921

The universe is awake
The heavenly sphere is dreaming
The planetary world is sleeping
The earthly being rests

Resting, the human being wakes
Sleeping, the human being feels
Dreaming, the human being wills
Awake, the human being becomes an I

I selve — I am
I will — I vanish
I feel — I become
I think — I am not — It is.

Notebook
July 1921

It speaks within
	I am
I speak to the outside
	It is
I feel on the outside
	It acts
I will out of my own-ness
	I act

Who wills in my own-ness?
What acts on the outside?
Who speaks to the outside?
Who speaks within?

In willing *I* know myself to be
On the outside that acts.

For Kristian Schjelderup
December 4, 1921

In
me
J deep Ch
down
divine ground
supporting
me

For Rudolf Meyer

I feel my I
I belong to humanity
I come from the soul realms
I use my power in the spheres of the spirit.

For Rudolf Meyer
December 1921

Imagine:

The light of the world streams through me too. —

May my prayer stream through the light of the world.

For Julia Marianne Wasteneys
1921

I say to Christ:

May your word be in my heart.

Christ says to me:

May my word be in your heart.

For Edith Rose Cull
August 31, 1922

May light overlight me
May love warm through me
I feel light
I feel warmth.

For Dorothy Osmond
1922

I seek the spirit
It comes forth from all things
It is in itself
It manifests out of itself —
World
Thought
        Me. —

Notebook, 1922

I let the water of the world solidify
Into crystal beads,
On which my thoughts are reflected —

I let my human fire flaming
Destroy itself in the will of the world.

Thus I hold myself in the balance
Between solidifying and blazing out,
Preserving my soul.

Notebook
February 1923

Light floods through the distances of space
World spirits, may you allow
My I to experience the pure world presence
Of the flooding light

Notebook, May 1923

When I plunge deeply into the force of thought
I touch the spiritual
When I lovingly take hold of a being
In the world darknesses
I feel the spiritual
When I with love take hold of a being
In the darknesses of the world
I think the spiritual.

Notebook, May 1923

To blend into the sea of existence with the death of space
To die into world being with the death of time
To experience oneself in the death of space and time

Notebook, May 1923

In my heart
Shines the force of the Sun
In my soul
Works the warmth of the world.

I want to breathe
The force of the Sun

I want to feel
The warmth of the world.

The force of the Sun fills me
The warmth of the world permeates me.

For a [female] French anthroposophist
1923

I am: The weight of the Earth works in me

I think: Breathing out, the human works in me

I feel: Breathing in, the human works into me

I will: The light of the universe works into me

Loose note sheet
c. 1923

1.) I gaze into the universe that my senses perceive, and that my mind, which is bound to my brain and nervous system, thinks about. Out of this universe comes what in me is body. It has its center in my limb system. What is spiritual there is only the will. But this will sleeps within me. I must awaken it.

2.) I think to myself: behind this universe is another universe, which my senses do not perceive and my mind cannot think about, because it is bound to my brain and nervous system. I existed in this other universe before I was born (conceived). I will exist in this other universe after I have died. From this other world come the forces that constructed the heart and lung system in my body. What is spiritual there is feeling. But this feeling dreams within me. I must understand what is dreaming in my feeling:

In each thing
In all becoming
    Dreams live;
In dreams I am,
Thinking disturbs me.
    May dreams live,
    Live in me —
In waking dreams,
Conscious and clear:
    As long as I live,
    There lives in me
    Strengthened by life
    A waking dream world.

The new reality,
Awakened by dreams,
I grasp
    In wakeful judgment.
It bears on its waves
The old reality
That showed me eyes,
That revealed to me ears,
That touched my skin.

The old reality
From you was awoken
Out of dreams,
You, new reality.

3.) I think to myself:
Both
the sense-reality
and the
Dream-awoken Reality
are in a
Third
Completely suprasensory, elevated, invisible,
ungraspable.
In this universe I am only
sleeping.
From this universe come the forces that
build spiritually my metabolic human being.
My intellect lives there.
In the human being
Who is there
Outside the physical-human
May spirit-being live;
I am in spiritbeing
But thinking disturbs me
Perceiving disturbs me
Feeling disturbs me
Willing disturbs me
Sleeping, I live
May there live in me
Spirit-world
Worlds-spirit —

So become conscious
Out of
Spirit-world
Worlds-spirit
Spirit-illuminated consciousness
Conscious light-spirit

The high reality
Sleep-awakened
I grasp with
Wakeful judgment
On its waves it bears
The old reality
That showed me eyes
And the new reality
That wove me dreams.

O high reality
Call my Self
To wakefulness
Let it forget
New reality
And old reality.

For Edith Maryon
c. 1923

Nr. 9.

Ganz langsam sollen die folgenden Vorstellungen durch das Gemüt ziehen:

Vor mir
In weiter Ferne
Steht ein Stern
Er kommt mir immer näher
Geistes=Wesen
Senden in Liebe
Mir Sternenlicht
Der Stern taucht ein
In mein eigenes Herz
Er füllet es mit Liebe
Die Liebe in meinem Herzen
Wird in meiner Seele
Kraft der Liebe
Ich weiss, dass ich
Auch in mir
bilden kann
die Kraft der Liebe.

The following ideas should pass slowly through the soul:

Before me
In the far distance
Stands a star
It draws ever closer to me
Spirit-being
In love send
Me starlight
The star dips down
Into my own heart
It fills it with love
In my soul
The love in my heart
Becomes in my soul
    Force of love
    I know that I
    can also form
    within myself
    the force of love.

For Yvonne Gygax-Kraft
1923

Meditation for attaining the I:

I look into the darkness:
In it light arises,
Living light.
Who is this light in the darkness?
I myself am it in my reality.
This reality of the I
Does not enter into my earthly existence.
I am only the image of it.
But I shall find it again,
When I,
Full of good will and effort for the spirit,
Have passed through the portal of death.

Lecture, London, September 2, 1923

I look into the darkness
Let light arise in it
Living light
Who is this light in the darkness
I myself am it
It did not come with me into earthly being
I am only the image of it
I will meet it again
When I have passed through the portal of death. —

Draft

The dust of the primordial force Sinks within me It arouses me	blue-black
The drops of the archangels Hover in me They give me life	blue
The fires of the angels Flame in me They shape me into soul	red
The drops of the archangels Hover in me They shape me into spirit.	yellow-red
The dust of the primordial force Rises within me It awakens me to God.	white-red

Notebook, September 1923

I take you into the Spirit Circle that may be referred to the impulses from the Sun Spirits and that may imply that the Moon Spirits transform these impulses into the Wisdom of the World.

Do you wish to hear my word from this spirit?

2	16	12	6	4	
o	o	o	o	o	
H	I	E	R	A	O

When you sense yourself in this word of the spirit,
the spirits of the Sun and Moon will know you.

They will allow themselves to be found by you; they would have to reject you, if you allowed this spirit word to fall from your heart. —

Imagine yourself sitting on the branch of a tree —
it holds you because your word is shining into the
spirit heights — falsely pronounced, you cut the
branch beneath you and you fall into the "abyss." —

Notebook
September 1923

I. Seek the seven everywhere, there is something of a spiritual kind, or something of a spiritual kind is happening.

II. Recognize, that, what is in the world is also in you, and that what is in you, is also in the world.

H i e r a o

♄ ♃ ♂ ☉ ♀ ☿

☾

III. Behold any spiraling disappear and appear again:

Loose note sheet
c. 1923

1. Into my I sinks warmth
   Given me from the source of being

   I awaken in the feeling of this warmth.

2. Into my body force radiates
   Coming to me from the Sun's force

   I awaken in the willing use of the Sun's force.

3. Into the life of my heart the Sun's light shines upon me
   Shining on me from the Sun's light.

   I awaken in the will of the Sun's being.

4. Into my being world thinking works
   Stirred in me by star-thoughts.

   I awaken magically in the thinking of the world.

Notebook
September 1923

What I speak out of my physical body is mere semblance —
I must speak out of my etheric body,
to penetrate true reality:

1. You spirits beneath the Earth press upon the soles of my feet.
   I walk over you and away.

2. You spirits of moisture stroke my skin.
   I push you to all sides.

3. You spirits of the air fill my inner depths.
   I unite myself with you.

4. You spirits of warmth ensoul my inner depths.
   I live in you.

5. You spirits of light permeate my inner depths with spirit.
   I think with you.

6. You spirits of [chemical] forces, lame my forces.
   I overcome you.

7. You spirits of life kill my life.
   I await you in death.

Thus, speaking this, I am in my etheric body.
Let all of you come: colors, sounds, words
of the etheric world.

For Ita Wegman
October 1923

Ever-shining, all-presiding light
I entrust my soul to you
May the light of my soul weave
In the weaving light of the world
I feel myself to be light
Light in little points
Light that extends itself to limitless expanses
Light that bears all of my being
Into limitless expanses
I feel myself in limitless expanses
I am pure transparent light

Notebook
October, 1923

I grasp the spirit world
At the end of my soul of light
I hold the spirit world
With my arms of light
I feel your side
You want to take me
Into the spirit worlds of light

Notebook
October, 1923

I look down
And find life supports
Through the good lower gods

I look up
And find the grace of life
Through the good upper gods

In gratitude to them I want
To find out of my heart
My way through life.

For Daniel van Bemmelen
January 3, 1924

In the name of the world's light,
Its waves shining through space;
In the name of the world's thought,
Creating wisely throughout time;
In the name of the world's life,
Functioning with power throughout eternity
Receive the blessing of the spirit

Which carries you in the heart's warmth,
Which brings you the breath of the spirit,
Which gives you the water of the soul,
Which shapes your bodily form;
That you may be strong in willing,
That you may live tenderly in feeling,
That you may act lucidly in thinking.

For Henry B. Monges
February 17, 1924

Cosmic light, which changes daily
Into the earthly light, and awakens human thinking;

Cosmic warmth, which long ago turned
Into earthly warmth, to live in human feeling;

Cosmic air, which before time began turned
Into earthly air, to act in human willing;

O human being, know yourself as a shining, warm spirit of
the heavens,
O human being, experience yourself as a true victor
Over the enticements of light, air, and warmth.

For Marie Steiner
March 15, 1924

I can know
That the thoughts
From the Goetheanum
Will be helping me.
I will think this
And take the hand
That will be given to me.

For Simone Rihouët-Coroze
May 23, 1924

Mornings and evenings.

In the expanses of the world
May soul-force act for all human beings
May spirit-might act all for all souls
  I want to breathe the force of the soul
  I want to feel the power of the spirit
  To be a God-permeated
    human being.

For Frau Renwald
July 1924

See, O my eye,
The Sun's pure rays
Out of theEarth's created beings;

See, O my heart,
The Sun's powerful spirit
Out of the water's pounding waves.

See, O my soul,
The Sun's world-will
Out of wind's shimmering gleaming;

See, O my spirit,
The Sun's divine beings of the Sun
Out of the fire's streams of love.

Notebook
September 1924

In the expanses of the world of space
Brightly shining light presides,
So that things reveal themselves;
In the depths of the human heart
Light becomes the force of thought,
So that souls can live.

Light of the heart and Light of the world:
In finding them may God live
In sacrificing human souls.
Thus may the human being waken
In the sensory world cycle. —

In the expanses of the spirit world
Sense-extinguishing darkness presides,
So that the spirit can announce itself;
In the life of the human soul
The darkness becomes the brightness of God,
So that human beings can breathe in the spirit.

Spirit of the soul and spirit of God's world:
In finding you a human being lives
In God's grace-bestowing work.
Thus sleeps the soul
In spirit's world cycle. —

If waking moves through the twilight of sleep,
And if sleeping moves through the brightness of waking,
Then the works of God will appear
In the world-sense-revelation.

For Pater Giuseppe Trinchero
September 9, 1924

A
In dir lebt das Menschenwesen
Das Gott von Angesicht zu Angesicht schauet, das ewig ist,
Und das im Kreise der sieben grossen Geister ist

B
Es ist über allem, was in dir
zornig oder furchtsam ist

c

G
Es herschet mit den Kräften der obern Welt
Und ihm dienen die Kräfte der untern Welt

i

D
Es verfügt über sein eigenes Leben und seine
eigene Gesundheit und kann das auch bei andern

o

H
Es kann durch nichts überrascht; von keinem Missgeschick
befallen werden; es kann nicht in Verwirrung gebracht und
nicht überwunden werden

u

V
Es kennt die Wesenheit des Vergangenen, Gegenwärtigen und Zukünftigen

Z
Es hat das Geheimnis der Erweckung vom Tode und von der Unsterblichkeit
im Besitz.

In you the human being lives
Who beholds God face to face, who is eternal,
And is in the circle of the seven great spirits

This being is above everything that in you
is angry or fearful

It rules with the forces of the upper world
and the forces of the lower world serve it

It orders its own life and its own health
and can also do so for others

Nothing can surprise it; no mischance can befall it;
It cannot be brought into a state of confusion and
it cannot be overcome

It knows the true nature of the past, present, and future

It possesses the secret of immortality and the awakening
from death.

Loose note sheet
c. 1924

For Johanna Mücke

In the heart
Lives a human organ
That of all the organs
Contains the most
Spiritual matter;
That of all organs
Lives spiritually
In such a way
That it manifests itself
The most materially.

Therefore the heart
Is the Sun
In the human universe;
Therefore it is in the heart
That the human being
In its being
Is most
In its deepest source —

On October 29, 1924

Sun, you bearer of rays,
The material power of your light
Conjures life out of the
Earth's immeasurably rich depths.

Heart, you bearer of souls,
The spirit power of your light
Conjures life out of humanity's
Immeasurably deep interiority.

If I look into the Sun
Its light speaks to me radiantly
Of the spirit, which filled with grace
Presides through the beings of the world.

If I feel in my heart
The spirit speaks its own word
About the human being,
Whom it loves through all time and eternity.

Looking upward I can see
In the Sun's bright round
The world's powerful heart.

Beholding inwards I can feel
In the heart's warm beat
The ensouled human Sun.

For Charlien Hupkes-Wegman
November 1924

If you look into the kingdom of your soul,
you can sense there
All the powers of light of the cosmic expanses
And God's activity over the course of time.

If you look into the kingdom of the Sun-world
You can see there
Your own heart's spirit-light
And creative work of your soul's forces.

Thus, in the heart's depths
The human soul can find delight
In the star worlds' heights,
And in the star worlds' heights
The human eye can find delight in
The spirit's weaving in the heart's depths. —

For Charlien Hupkes-Wegman
November 1924

For my dear Marie as a meditation,
not for a particular time of day, but at your leisure.
Christmas 1924

In starry expanses
To the places of the gods
My soul
Turns its spirit gaze.

Out of starry expanses
From the places of the gods
Streams the force of the spirit
Into my soul.

For starry expanses
Toward the places of the gods
My spirit heart lives
Through my soul.

For Marie Steiner

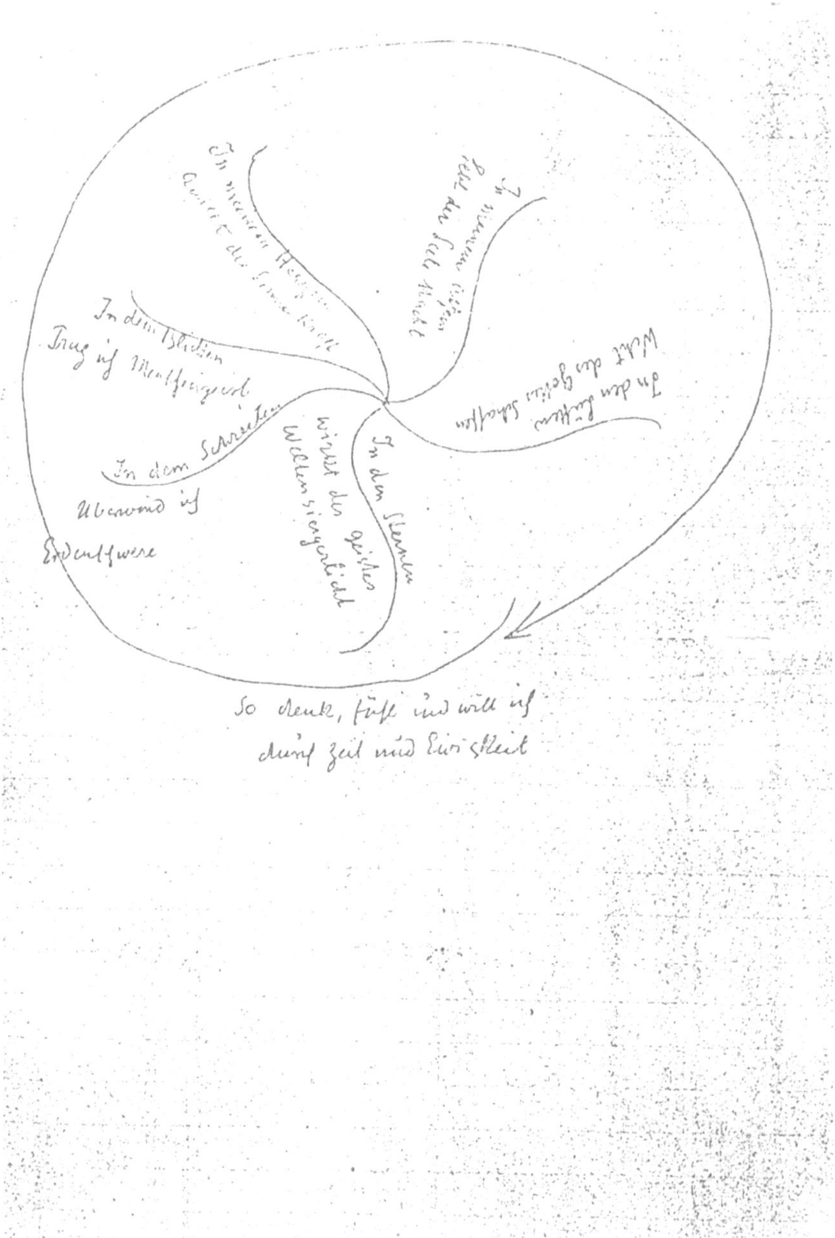

In walking
I overcome Earth's heaviness

In looking
I bear the human spirit

In my heart
Wells the Sun's force

In my breath
Lives the soul's power

In the breezes
Wafts God's creative work

In the stars
Spirit's world-victorious light is at work

Thus I think, feel, and will
Through time and eternity.

For Hans Werner Zbinden
1924

In my aura
I see
With the eye of Michael
With the strength of Christ
With the power of consecration:
How the divine-spiritual
Presides
In me.

———

From upper places of the worlds
The divine-spiritual
Radiates through me;

The stars
from above
bear the divine-spiritual
through me

From the far perimeter of the worlds
The divine-spiritual
Rolls in waves through me.

The Sun
Circling around
Sinks the divine-spiritual
Into me

Out of the deep clefts in the Earth
The divine-spiritual
Streams through me.

The Earth
From below
Supports the divine-spiritual
In me.

Loose note sheet
1924

Find yourself in the light
With the soul's own tone;
And the tone vaporizes
Becomes a color image
          In the light —
Light — gods — beings.

Vanished tone
In it resurrected tone
     Speaks out of it:

          You are

Your own tone in the light of the worlds
     Radiant tones
     Radiate sounding.

Notebook
1924

Seraphisch Feuermächte
aus meinem Herzen strahlet
Cherubinisch Bildekräfte
In meinem Haupte scheinet
Der Throne Traggewalten
In meinen Gliedern
Kraftlicher

Mein Ich ist IHR

Fire powers of the Seraphim
You radiate from my heart

Image forces of the Cherubim
You shine in my head

Bearing powers of the Thrones
You work in my limbs

My I is YOURS.

Eurythmy Form

Loose note sheet
1924

To feel oneself in the head
To seek the way into etheric worlds
To sense oneself in the word
Leads into worlds of the soul
To experience the radius of the hands
To penetrate into the realm of the spirit
Thus I find myself in the universe.

Loose note sheet
Undatable

To the sign of the cosmic spirit
My yearning soul lifts itself
⋮

In the bright light of the shining rose
I glimpse the power of the spirit.

In the deep foundation of my soul
The same spiritual power awakens
Let it carry, hold, guide me.

Loose note sheet
Undatable

The Sun shines
In the darkness of matter;
So shines the spirit's
All-healing being
Into the darkness of the soul
In my human existence.
As often as I recall
Its strong power
In true warmth of heart
It shines through me
With its spiritual noonday power.

Undatable

My soul follows the light of the Sun
My soul is a being of light
Following the Sun
My soul as light finds the light.

For Wilhelm Selling
Undatable

Sun above me
Sun in the heavenly blue
I on the Earth-Star
Green shines the Earth
In the cosmic distances
Plant-green gives the Earth
A uniform green as star-color
Divine powers of metal
Deep within the homes of the gnomes
Color the star blossoms
Red, blue, yellow
On the green ground of the plant-star.

Loose note sheet
Undatable

From the stars I have climbed down.
To the stars I will raise myself up.
I will act with Michael.
I will live for Christ.

For Alfred Meebold
Undatable

In deepest human inwardness
Is the firm midpoint
In all life's situations
One can build upon the spirit
That dwells in this midpoint.

For Edith Brend Lewis
Undatable

In the spirit the being of the human is rooted
In the spirit, the true life force is hidden
May my heart cling to the spirit
Thus in myself I find myself.

For a [male] Finnish anthroposophist
Undatable

In quiet struggle
In light-striving
Soul life
My I bears
Me toward the source
From which human beings
Create their being (essence). —

Loose note sheet
Undatable

You seek
For the light of the spirit world:
Seek it in your own self,
And you will certainly find it.

You seek
Your own self-being:
Seek it in the working of the world,
And you will certainly find it.

The darkness of one's own being:
Darkens the world.
To be unaware
Of the working of the world
Chills the individual self.

For Hans Hasso von Veltheim
Undatable

World-beings unite
As soul-building forces
Creative of thought
In my heart
They find themselves
In spiritual activity
With goodness of will
In the human I.

Goodness of will streams
Into the human I
Following spiritual activity
To illuminate itself
In my heart
In the force of world-thought
Soul-bright
To find the world's essence.

Loose note sheet
Undatable

Know yourself
Power is in your heart
Strength is in your soul
Seek strength through the soul
Seek power through the heart
The power that in you says:
Know yourself.

Know yourself
The power that in you says:
Seek power through the heart
Seek strength through the soul
Strength is in your soul
Power is in your heart
Know yourself.

Undatable

I feel
Power in my hands
Strength in my feet

I feel
Love in my heart
Light in my head

I feel
God's soul in my breath
God's will in my speech
God's spirit in my sensing.

Undatable

Imagination of a triangle made of three stars. From the first, streams love; from the second, power; from the third, wisdom.

☆ Love (red)

☆ Power (blue) ☆ Wisdom (yellow)

Then meditate on:

To work in love
To quicken oneself by power
To strive in wisdom
    May this fulfill my I [I-CH].

This may be repeated several times during the day.

Undatable

Whoever wants to know God, must want God — Will

Whoever is to know the
Logos must feel the Logos — Love

Whoever is to know the spirit must
think the spirit — Light

Whoever wishes to advance humanity
must find the fire — Fire

Loose note sheet
Undatable

Within me I bear what has been,
Within me I feel what is becoming,
Willing I bear both toward the future.

Faith looks on what has been and is founded in the truth,
Trust looks at what is coming and is founded in the future,
Love encompasses in an instant
The eternally becoming
The eternally being.

Undatable

Inhaling, think:

The highest force of nature streams
Into me with the breath.

Holding the breath:

All power rests within me.

Exhaling:

I stream out all the good
Of which I am capable

Undatable

I inhale the force of life from the blue distances.

I exhale my own self into the blue distances.

Loose note sheet
c. 1923

	I	II	III
gleichzeitig	Die Welt giebt mir den Atem physisch lebend	Der Atem lebet und stirbt in mir zu Geist	Den erstorbenen ergeistigten Atem gebe ich der Welt
	einatmen	atem gehalten	ausatmen
	Ich	bin	Ich

I

The world gives me breath living physically

II

The breath lives and dies in me into spirit

III

To the dead I give enspirited breath to the world

I am I

Note: The following is not in Rudolf Steiner's handwriting:
down the left side, referring to "I am I": *"simultaneously"*
below I: "inhaling"; below II "holding the breath"; below III, "exhaling."

Loose note sheet
Undatable

MEDITATIONS FOR THE DAYS OF THE WEEK

Verses for the days of the week are also in the volumes of the Esoteric Lessons, CW 266/vols. 1-3.

Life flows, born of the One,
formless free particles,
suspended in particles, particle
animating particle. — Sunday

It allows directing forces, delineating forms
speeding from chaos through space
giving birth to order, releasing
determination into chaos. — Monday

It forms shapes, structures
beings, allows the yearning to develop
that impels beings toward beings, allows
selfhood to become, that separates being
from being. — Tuesday

It allows being to tend lovingly to being,
gives birth to relationship and unity, maintaining
selfhood, pouring self into piety, creatively
forming selfhood above oneself. — Wednesday

[It] allows created form Thursday
to enrich itself with wisdom, as
wisdom fluidly creating birth and grave in
eternal becoming. — Friday

[It allows created form ?]
to sink down to a being, waking memory,
arousing an urge to deeds — sheltering the divine,
so that the divine might arise. — Saturday

It is it	Sunday	I love myself
It thinks it	Monday	I am I
It wills it	Tuesday	I think myself
It loves it	Wednesday	I will myself

It is I	Thursday
It thinks me	Friday
It wills me	Saturday

Draft
Notebook, 1902/03

Saturday:

The good and bad lots for my soul rest quietly
in the womb of the future.

Sunday:

What good flows daily to me, I will notice;
by it I am shown,
what gods make out of me.

Monday:

What bad sometimes flows to me, I want to bear;
by it I am shown,
what I can still make of myself.

Tuesday:

I thank my good fate for the way
I live now.

Wednesday:

> I thank my strength in
> challenging situations for the force that
> can lead me upward in life.

Thursday:

> Whoever believes that only good fate advances us,
> and that only bad things bring us down,
> does not see the year, but only the day.

Friday:

For Emma Gétaz
1910

Saturday mornings:

May the beauty of the world stream into me.

Sunday mornings:

I will.

Notebook, 1910

Saturday:

I find the warmth in the universe
as the joy of creative workin my soul

Sunday:	Light	Thinking
Monday:	Harmony	Mood (Contentment)
Tuesday:	Life	Sense of Self
Wednesday:	Air	Will
Thursday:	Water	Feeling
Friday:	Earth	Knowledge

Notebook, 1910

Sunday:

Light: symbol of wisdom

Monday

Warmth: symbol of love

Tuesday:

Breath: symbol of the spirit penetrating into me.

Wednesday:

My blood moves within me
In the universe of the elements.

Thursday:

As the clouds bless the Earth
The grace of the spirit blesses me.

Friday:

In waking, my soul appears as
Pure as the morning Sun.

Saturday:

For Emilie Anderson
June 7, 1913

Saturday:

If I say to myself:
Have courage, my soul,
Then I say what is true in the spirit
Even if the outer world sometimes shows something different.

Sunday:

Everyone's higher self
Watches over their karma

Monday:

Everyone's higher self
Speaks invisibly with their angel

Tuesday:

In the three sayings
I will be able to find direction for my thinking.

Wednesday:

God's power rests in me
I will surely find it

Thursday:

The human being lives from darkness into brightness

Friday:

Harmony is in the spiritual.

Loose note sheet
After 1914

First day:

Presiding in peace, O invisible begetter of the world,
illuminate my will through my thinking.

Second day:

Living in love, O palpable preserver of the world,
take my will as a sacrifice.

Third day:

Fulfiller of the whole world, O you, showing yourself everywhere
revealer of the world, fulfill me too.

Loose note sheet
Undatable

Saturday:

I lead my soul

Sunday:

Divine light around my soul

Monday:

Rest in the spirit is the force of existence

Tuesday:

Energetic thinking gives confidence in eternal being

Wednesday:

Always be true to yourself, my soul

Thursday:

Know yourself from your feeling and actions

Friday:

To gather the force of life is always courageous

Loose note sheet
After 1914

Sunday:

Spirit of the world, enter into my heart,
into my soul, into my I.

Monday:

I look to you, spirit of the world,
I give myself to you with my heart,
my soul, and my I.

Tuesday:

I must feel you, spirit of the world,
feel you from deepest within,
with my heart, my soul,
my I.

Wednesday:

By your mercy I wind myself
from step to step, to the heights strive
my heart, my soul, my I.

Thursday: 

In YOUR light I must become healthy,
strong, and fearless in ------ *

Friday:

I am in you, spirit of the world,
and your gifts are in me.

Saturday:

I AM

For Lotus Peralté
Undatable

*Footnote: "The esotericist falls silent in word and thought when the Holy Name, the inexpressible, should be named"— Esoteric lesson in Cologne, January 2, 1913. See CW 266/III, *Esoteric Lessons III.*

Saturday:

The light that brightens space
should count as the symbol of wisdom.

Sunday:

The warmth that warms an object
should count as the symbol of love.

Monday:

A being that breathes, proves,
that it can only exist as part of the air world.

Tuesday:

A being that cognizes, proves,
that it can only exist as part of the spirit world.

Wednesday:

By breathing out, a being shows
that the inner becomes the outer in existence.

Thursday:

Human judgment is in the spiritual realm
what breathing out is in the physical realm.

Friday:

If I say: I am, then the spirit,
by means of which I am, affirms itself in me.

For Rudolf Hah
Undatable

Saturday:

I consecrate my heart to the strong forces of the cosmos:
feeling warmth in my heart

Aux fortes puissances du cosmos je consacre mon cœur
(sentir chaleur dans le cœur)

Sunday:

I consecrate my head to the streaming forces of the cosmos
feeling light in my head

Aux rayonantes puissances du cosmos je consacre ma tête
(sentir lumière dans la tête)

Monday:

I consecrate myself wholly to the warming forces of the cosmos
feeling strength in all of my limbs

Aus réchauffantes puissances du cosmos je me consacre toute entière
(sentir force dans tous les members)

For Emma Gétaz
Undatable

FOR STRENGTHENING THE LIFE FORCES

May my heart and soul be filled

Peace	Rest	○
Rest	Strength	△
Strength	Hope	♂

Imagine the figures after the words
(Do this as often as you find yourself needing to do it.)

Mi riempi cuore e l'anima

Pace	Calma	○
Calma	Forza	△
Forza	Speranza	♂

Rappresentarsi le figure dopo le parole
(Far questo esercizio tante volte quanto se ne sente il bisogno.)

For Giovanni Colazza
c. 1910

May God's power solicitously watch always over me
May the power of God always solicitously watch over me

Moving, may the life of the spirit flow into me
Flowing into me may the life of the spirit be moving

I in feeling and thinking
Thinking and feeling in the I.

For Auguste Daeglau
1910

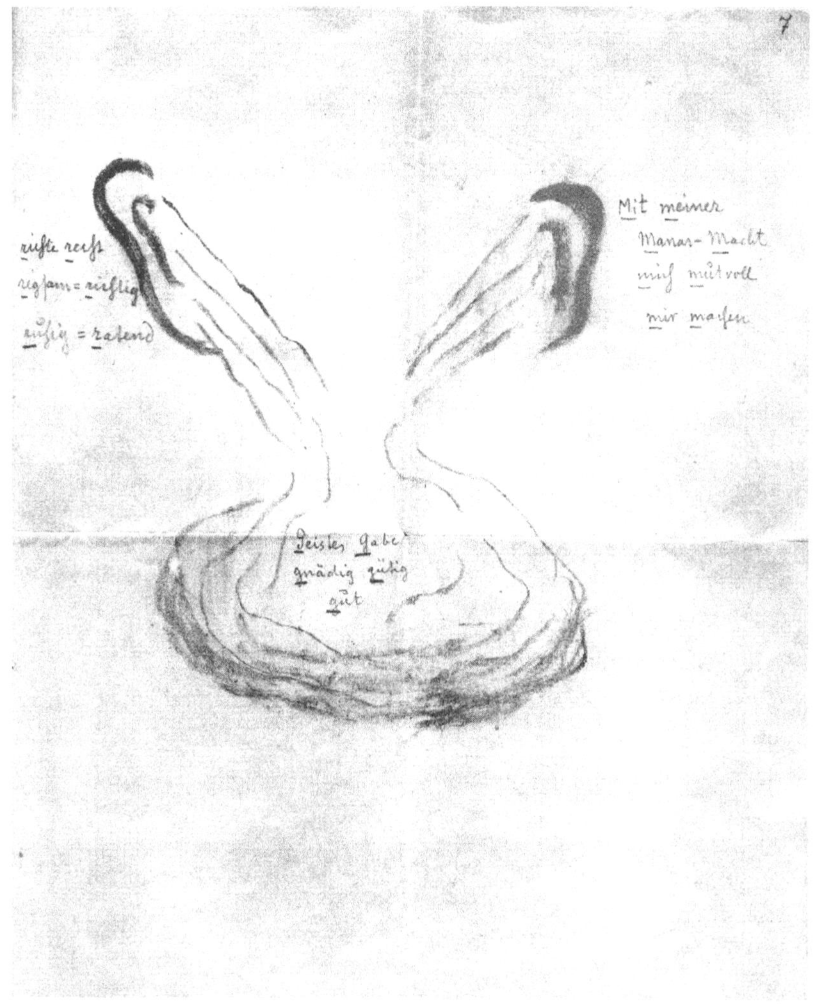

The sketch is colored:

left: greenish-blue	judge right / alert correct / quiet advising
middle: violet	spirit gift / gracious kind-hearted / good
right: red	with my / Manas-Power / me courageous / make me

For Lucie Bürgi
c. 1910

Light around me
Light fill me
Light strengthen me
Light free me
Light place me
  Upon myself
    I

For Friedrich Krüger
1911/12

In the ground of the world
There rest for me
Strengthening me
Warming world becoming beings
Anticipate peace, attaining in the right way
My heart, practiced in waiting,
Your being's becoming.

For Hilde Boos-Hamburger
November 1912

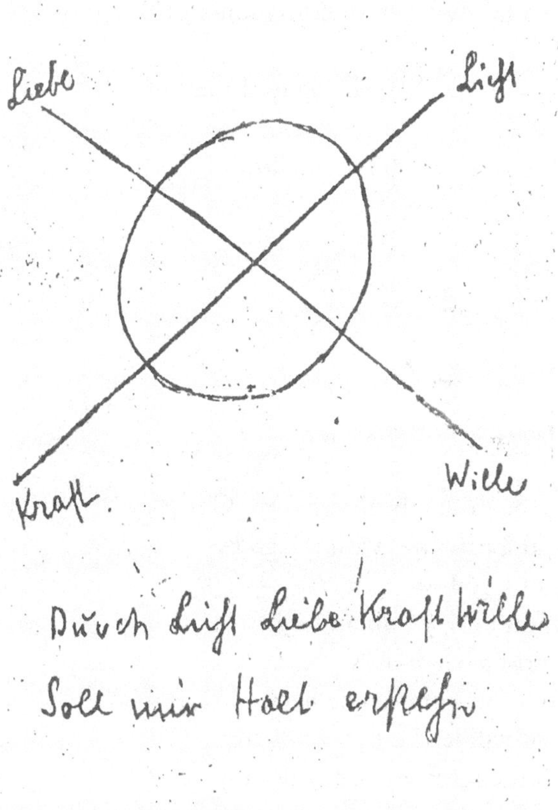

Through light love strength will
Support will arise for me

For Ernst Kober
1912

I seek to feel in my head sounding tones of the spirit.

I seek to feel in my chest the light of the spirit.

I seek to feel all through me the flow of the spirit.

For Elisabeth Maier
1914

If we do not accept our destiny

In the primal beginning was Christ,
And Christ was with the gods,
And a god was Christ.
And in every human soul
Christ's being lives.
So in my soul too he lives
And will lead me
To the meaning of my destiny.

For a worker who is going deaf
c. 1919/20

To you, the divine in my soul,
I want to give space
In my conscious being:
You connect me to everything
That the power of destiny has brought to me
You will never release me
From what you have given
Me to love:
Your spirit watches over mine
Because it is also yours:
Thus I will watch with you,
Through you, in you,
What you have decided to do with what is yours.
I want to be strong, to know
That this is wisdom. —

For Olivia Römer
Christmas 1919

May power shine through me
Strength sound through me
Shine and sound through
My legs and arms
Shine and sound through
My hands and feet
Thus will I become powerful
Thus will I become strong
Strong and powerful
In heart and head
Powerful and strong
In breath and speech.

Notebook, 1920

In my heart I find strength,
In my head I find understanding,
If I think about this,
I can strengthen myself
In all my limbs and organs.
I shall do it.
Do it with all my might.

For twelve-year-old Felicitas Stückgold
1921

Christ, from within I will become you
With pure, true understanding

I look to you
You live in me

I live through you
You stream through me
Thus I may trust
And always build

My own better being
To heal completely.

Notebook, 1921

In the morning:

I see before me a white wall,
On it I write:
I am.

I step upon a blue surface,
Right foot: I press the floor
Left foot: The floor supports me

I am surrounded by the red-yellow firmament
The firmament encircles me and warms me
I breathe in: *i*
I hold my breath: *a*
I breathe out: *o*

At midday:

God's wisdom orders the world —
And orders me too;
I will live in that wisdom.
God's love warms the world —
It warms my heart too;
I want to breathe in that love.
God's strength carries the world —
It carries my body too;
I want to think in it.

In the evening:

It grows dark
My soul goes into the darkness
It will illuminate the darkness,
Illuminate it, because the wisdom, strength, and goodness of
the divine is in my soul;
Wisdom, strength, and goodness
Grow in my soul in the darkness —
By means of these, full of life,
My soul will glow again
Through head, heart, and limbs. —

For Maria Elsässer
Summer 1921

Mornings:

Beaming Sun-star
Glowing native house
World-forming being
Open for me
Heart and soul-understanding
So that I may be strong
In time and eternity.

Evenings:

To dwell in the spirit
And to breathe spiritually
Is the soul's instinct
It comes to me
When sleeping
When my eye
Protecting itself closes itself.

For Mrs. Roberts
November 1921

I hear the Sun-word
It speaks
May light shine heart-light
Into your heart
Strengthen your human power
You will become healthy
Through the Sun-word.

For Alcibiade Mazzarelli
June 11, 1922

Into my head, glowing, warming
Spirit Light pours itself
Warming me, it presses its way
Into my heart
I feel it stream
Into all my limbs
And unite me with God's—Cosmic—All.

Loose note sheet
c. 1923

Between 11 and 1: I see myself walk around myself.
Evenings, before sleep: I walk around myself.
Mornings:

> Human beings bear within
> their eternal spirit
> The eternal spirit
> Is planted
> In the divinity of the world
> I rest in the divinity of the world
> I will find myself in the divinity of the world.

For Hans Olsen
May 19, 1923

I feel sunlight in my heart
Sunlight becomes warmth in my heart
My heart force streams into my hands
My heart force streams into my feet
My heart force is a gift from God
I will work with God's gift
Thus may I hope to become strong.

(Then become quite peaceful in your soul)

Loose note sheet
May 19, 1923

May warmth surround me

The light, it shines into my head
With quiet force
I sense it

The air, it streams into my chest
With quiet force
I breathe it

Gravity, it holds me to the Earth
With quiet force
I experience it

In light, air, and gravity
Sensing, breathing, experiencing
May my entire human self be woven

May warmth surround me

For thirteen-year-old Rolf Gutbrod
1923

Sunrise in the evening one-half minute
then:

The light of the Sun
Works before me
Becomes warmth
Enters into my heart
Streams through me
I am
In warmth. —

Sunset in the morning one-half minute

I am in warmth
Warmth moves
Out of my body
Into my heart
I give
The warmth
To the light (the Sun). —

For Ingeborg Zeylmans
c. 1923

I feel in my head
the warm force of love

I feel in my heart
the shining might of thought

The warm force of love
Unites itself with the
Shining might of thought

From this my hands
Grow strong
For good human works.

I feel myself.

For Mrs. C. A. Bergsma
c. 1923

Lying down: Think of the inside of your head —
as if warmth radiated there,
add the words:

Forcefully
From my head streams
Warmth
Through my chest
Through my arms
Through my legs
And may it strengthen me.

Loose note sheet, 1923

Meditation:

above: red
middle: red-blue
below: blue

the red warms
the blue cools

In the spirit hear: prime — minor third — fifth

three times one after the other
seven times

Loose note sheet, c. 1923

I find myself in myself
Divine power grasps me
In the radius of my being
I grasp divine power
In the middle of my heart
Thus I find my spirit
Giving
Peace, peace, peace
To my soul yearning for God.

For Friedrich Wilhelm von Flotow
1924

Evenings:

True to yourself you will become strong.

Mornings:

True to myself I will become strong. —

For Andreas von Grunelius
c. 1924

What life from its depths
Has decided to set before my spirit
From the sources of world destiny —
The brave soul finds
The right path when it
Trusts the bright warm I. —

For Walter Johannes Stein
February 18, 1924

1.) Quiet calm spreads throughout my whole soul realm.

2.) Gratefully I accept what the spirit wishes to reveal to me.

3.) I would like to be able to be imperturbable, calm and composed, so that karma can shape from what I have seen and experienced what should become through me.

For Walter Johannes Stein
March 1924

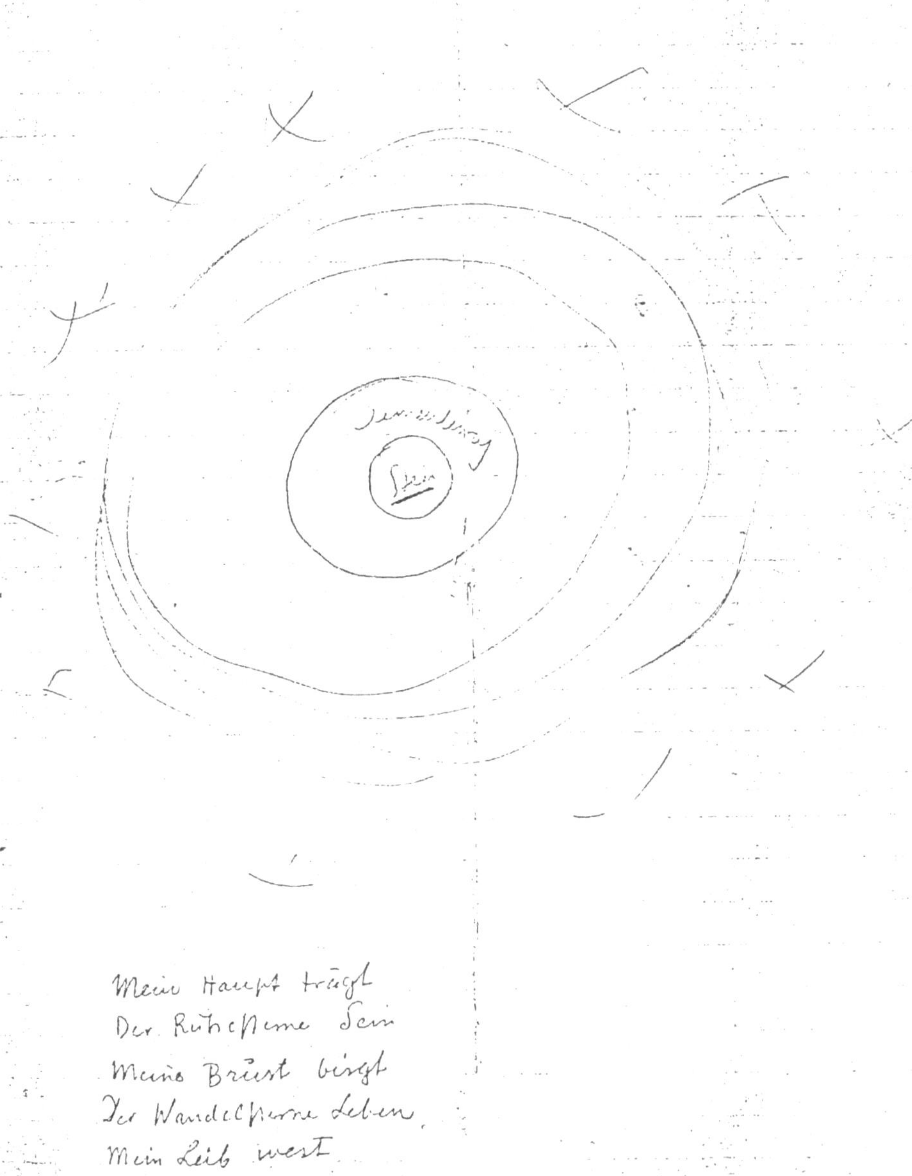
Sein
Mein Haupt trägt
Der Ruhesterne Sein
Meine Brust birgt
Der Wandelsterne Leben
Mein Leib west
Im Elementenwesen

In the center of the very faded sketch:

Stein - Stone / Path of the Elements

[*Elementeweg* or *Elementenreich*] / Realm of the Elements

My head bears
The being of the fixed stars
My breast contains
The life of the wandering stars
My life exists
In the existence of the elements
That I am.

For Walter Johannes Stein
April 1924

Mornings:

In my heart
Dwells the force
That enlivens me
If I grasp it
With my will
It will carry me
In health through life

Evenings:

If I look around me
I see the Sun's
Deeds of light
If I look into myself
I see the soul's
Spirit will
I am light in the spirit
Spirit in light.

Loose note sheet
March 1924

The stars are shining
It is night
Peaceful quiet fills space
Everything is silent
I feel peace
I feel silence
In my heart
In my head
God speaks
Christ speaks.

For ten-year-old Nik Fiechter
June 1924

Tranquil blue all around me
Quiet peace in my soul
The spirits of the universe speak:

Let stars shine
In your human body;
Shining stars,
Warming stars.

For Emmy Thurnheer
August 1924

O my soul, quickened by the spirit,
May the most beautiful forces of my I
Carry me sunward
You take up the Sun's force
Into the creative forces of the human being
In your own being
Altogether kindheartedly. —

For Mrs. Stumpe
September 1924

Hold the breath for a long time;
before that, an imagination of the Sun:

My light
Permeate evenings
Your soul.

Moon:

Your beams
Permeate mornings
My soul.

Note, 1924

May you be, my heart
Bearer of the soul
Home of my divine being
Which, leading me, lives with me
Giving light
Bringing warmth
In time and eternity.

For Mrs. Machesini
1924

Le soir:

Mon cœur
Reçois la grâce du Christ
Veuille échauffer mon âme,
Esprit dans mon sang
Veuille éclairer mon esprit
que je devienne
ferme et sain
Pour le travail dans le monde.

Le matin:

Mon âme
Tu dois ressentir la grâce du Christ
De mon cœur
Christ me tient
Dans le pays de l'esprit
Et me donne
La force pour la vraie vie.

In the evening:

  My heart
Receive the grace of Christ
Warm my soul
Spirit in my blood
Illumine my spirit
So that I may become
Strong and healthy
For work in the world.

In the morning:

  My soul
You must feel the grace of Christ
In my heart
Christ holds me
In the land of the spirit
And gives me
Strength for true life.

Two loose note sheets, 1924

Mornings:

A white beam
Of the bright Sun
Falls into my heart
I grow stronger
Through the white beam
Thrice it strengthens
My I —

Evenings:

Darkness,
Spirit darkness
Takes me up

Out of the darkness
I will
Receive the light
The bright-dark light. —

For Hedwig Linnhoff
1924

Blue firmament,
Deep blue,
Star-bedecked.

The Moon goes thither,
Gentle light comes from it,
Gentle light enters my brow,
Moonlight.

The Sun sends it,
The Moon makes it gentle,
May it make me healthy.

Undatable

May there descend
From the vastness of the world,
The wise working force of spirit
That I seek yearningly
In my soul's speech
And may it bear, lead, and hold me
In myself through itself.

Undatable

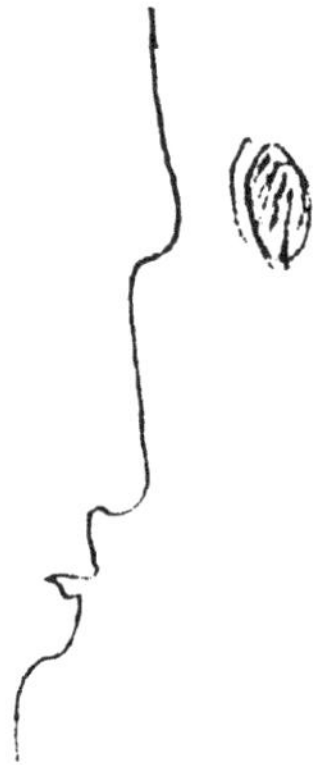

Left eye: Into me works the force of the world breath

Thoughtful inhalation
Thoughtful exhalation

Right eye: Out of me works the force of the human breath

World breath and human breath
Are the pulse-beats of God.

For Tessa Rosenkrantz
Undatable

I bear tranquility within me,
I bear within me
The forces that strengthen me.
I will fill myself
With the warmth of these forces,
I will permeate myself
With the might of my will.
And I will feel
How tranquility pours
Through my entire being
When I strengthen myself
To find within me
Tranquility as strength
Through the might of my striving.

For Miriam Ege
Undatable

O divine spirit fill me,
Inspire me in my soul;
Give strength to my soul,
And strength to my heart,
To my heart, which seeks you,
Seeks through deep longing,
Deep longing for health,
For health and fortitude,
Fortitude, so that I can become useful,
Become useful for life.

Note
Undatable

Divine spirit within me
Seeking inner peace within me
Inner peace that lives in all my limbs
In all the limbs that join together my body
My body that my soul quickens
My soul that my spirit illuminates
My spirit that the divine spirit inspires.

Note
Undatable

O spirit of God fill me
Inspire me in my soul;
Lend to my soul strong force,
And strong force to my heart, too
To my heart that seeks you,
Seeks through deep longing
Deep longing for health
For health and fortitude
Courage that streams into my limbs
Streams like a divine gift
A divine gift from you, O spirit of God
O spirit of God, fill me.

Note
Undatable

I think of my heart
It quickens me
It warms me
I trust steadfastly
In the eternal self
That works in me
That carries me. —

Note
Undatable

In me the force of warmth
I feel the force of warmth,
It penetrates me
Penetrates from my head through my heart
Through my whole body

I feel myself warmed through and through. —

Note
Undatable

May courage stream from the heart
To the painful places
And warming alleviate suffering.

For Wilma Schreiber
Undatable

Thinking of the left foot

My I bears me

Thinking of the right foot

My I holds me

Thinking of the left hand

My I protects itself

Thinking of the right hand

My I defends itself

Bearing force
Holding force
Protection and defense
I make these four
into one
in my heart.

For Maria Schröfel
Undatable

You must now say:

I want to be strong
I want to be strong in my hands
I want to be strong in my heart
May God help me
That I may become strong
I pray to God
That He may strengthen my hand
I pray to God
That He may strengthen my heart
Then I will be strong.

For Louis Olivier
Undatable

Now I lay myself down to rest
I am at peace
I hear myself
At rest I hear myself
In a state of great stillness I hear myself
  I remain at rest

— One and a half hours —

  My rest is over
  I begin again
    To move myself.

For Clarita Benkendörfer
Undatable

Meditation with the Rose Cross

I

The cross, as if arising out of burning wood. Then, on it, reddish, peeling off, the seven roses, which gradually become bright and glowing.

1. First rose, lighting up: left half of the head
   May your warmth warm me through —

2. Second rose, lighting up: right half of the head
   May your light illuminate me —

3. Third rose, lighting up: left hand
   May your activity stream through me —

4. Fourth rose, lighting up: right hand
   May your peace flow through me —

5. Fifth rose, lighting up: left foot
   May the force of your ray empower me —

6. Sixth rose, lighting up: right foot
   May your uplifting permeate me —

7. Seventh rose, lighting up: above
   I am in your sphere.

II

Flow powerfully through me,
Flow actively streaming,
Streaming from below upward,
Above, strengthening itself in the spirit,
Strengthening itself through the source of life,
The source of life that came down,
Came down from its Sun existence
        Through me.

For Suse Karstens
Undatable

Mornings:

I have been drawn from the intangible
Into the tangible.
I lived in the spirit
When I slept without sensation.
When I awake feeling
I live in the senses.
I should call divine
Both the intangible and the tangible.
In God I am awake,
And even when I am sleeping I am
In God,
From whom I come,
To whom I am going.

Evenings:

> To God
> I am going
> From whom I have come.
> In him I am sleeping,
> In him I am waking.
> I should call divine
> Both the tangible and the intangible.
> I live in the senses,
> When I wake in feeling.
> I live in the spirit,
> When I sleep without feeling.
> Through sleep
> I am drawn into the intangible.
> The intangible is
> In the spirit.
> Sleeping, I shall be
> In the spirit.

For a blind young boy
Undatable

In danger of death

You spirit of my life, protective companion,
Be goodness of heart in my willing,
Be human love in my feeling,
Be light of truth in my thinking.

Undatable

TO PROVIDE HELP FOR OTHERS

I sink myself into the deepest soul forces within me,
I live there, feeling, in my soul, in the eternal.
As the point lives in the circle without expanding,
Even so does the eternal soul live within me without a bodily being.

With this bodiless eternal being I remember
helping in the spirit — — — [name of person]

May the strength to be yourself strengthen in you the light
That shines in your own interiority: may it enliven itself in you.
May the soul warmth, raying from your own spirit,
Warm you through and through. —

Note
Undatable

Thoughts, spirit-grown
Make their way
From my soul to yours
So that they may work
Filling with life out of the spirit
What you strive for in your own way
In your heart's soul-ground.

Note,
Undatable

May he learn to feel
In his soul his forces
Knowing himself
In these forces
To feel himself beating in his heart
To know himself thinking in his head
To know himself feeling in his body.

To Clara Walberg for her son
1909

May the beings you long for spiritually accompany you in your striving. May they take hold of your thoughts and allow their thoughts to flow into yours, so that you will feel and experience them in your thoughts. May they flow into your sensing; and uniting yourself with them, may you add yourself to the worlds you aspire to.

Loose note sheet
c. 1910

Hearts that love,
Suns that warm,
Traces of the way of Christ
In the Father's universe —
We call to you from our own breast,
We seek you in our own spirit,
  O may we strive toward him!

Rays from the human heart,
Longing warmed with devotion,
Christ's native places
In the Father's earthly house—
We call to you from our own breast,
We seek you in our own spirit,
  O may we live with him!

Glowing human love,
Warming glimmer of the Sun,
Soul-garment of Christ
In the Father's human temple —
We call to you from our own breast,
We seek you in our own spirit,
  O may we help in him!

For a very sick man
February, 1925

MEDITATIONS GIVEN DURING THE FIRST WORLD WAR

Blood source,
Work in flowing;
Active muscle,
Move the seeds;
Loving care
Of the warming heart
Be healing breath.

The Samaritan Course
Lecture, Dornach, August 13, 1914

As long as you feel pain
That avoids me
Christ remains unrecognized
In cosmic being;
For weak is the spirit
That can feel suffering
Only in its own body.

The Samaritan Course
Lecture, Dornach, August 14, 1914

Everything that has been said may now be condensed into seven lines; seven lines that can help you achieve what has been portrayed as a Christ-imbued mutual conversation with the folk spirit:

You, spirit of my earthly space,
Unveil the light of your Age
Of Christ-gifted souls,
That striving they may find
In the choir of the spheres of peace,
Echoing you with praise and power
Of Christ-devoted human minds.

The Samaritan Course
Lecture, Dornach, August 16, 1914

You, spirit of my earthly place
Pour forth your light
From your Age
Into my questioning soul
That it may find
Its spiritual place
In human brotherly union.

Draft

From the mercy-bestowing soul of the world
May the force of warmth fill me
The warmth that passes through
Human beings
As God's power passes through
The wide, wide universe.

Prayer for the very ill
given to Helene Röchling
1914/15

Wholly into your soul
Into your thinking, feeling, and willing
With the fire-force of Yahweh
May the working being of my soul
Filled with Christ, dip down into your soul
And lead into your being *Elohimic* fire-will
So that deed of life glows from it.

Stand before me, take
spirit-touching—soul-peace maintaining
Strongly given
Soul-warm
Heart-quickened
Christ-sacrificed
Life-help, being-with-you.

Draft for
"I want to believe...,"
Notebook 1914

I w i l l believe you,
M a y I know you,
In the protection of the spirit,
That broods there over the middle of Europe
Over his people, the aim of his spirit;
May he guide toward you the force of Yahweh's thinking
May he give you will from the source of Christ's will.

Given to Helene Röchling
1914

I w i l l believe
M a y I know you
In the protection of the spirit
Who broods over the middle of Europe
Over the people, its spirit's goal
May it lead to you my faith in Yahweh
May it lovingly give you my power-of-knowing Christ.

Given to Eliza von Moltke
1914

Aus dem Mut der Kämpfer
Aus dem Blut der Schlachten
Aus dem Leid Verlassener
Aus des Volkes Opfertaten
Wird erwachsen Geistesfrucht,
Lenken Seelen geist=bewusst
Ihren Sinn ins Geisterreich.

From the courage of warriors
From the blood of battles
From the sorrow of those left behind
From the people's sacrificial deeds
Spiritual fruit shall grow
Spirit-conscious souls shall lead
Their understanding into the spirit realm.

From September 1914

From the sorrow of the souls
From the blood of the battles
From the sense of sacrifice and courage for battle
From the pain, suffering, and death
Spiritual fruit shall grow
Spirit-conscious human beings shall lead
Their souls' understanding toward the spirit.

Draft

For those who remain standing on the battlefield

Spirits of your souls, active watchers,
May your efforts bring to our souls
Supplicating love
Protection to earthly humans close to you,
So that, united with your power,
Our plea may helping shine
On the souls who seek it lovingly.

For those who have fallen on the battlefield

Spirits of your souls, active watchers,
May your efforts bring to our souls
Supplicating love
Protection to those in human spheres close to you
So that, united with your power,
Our plea may helpfully shine
On souls who seek it lovingly.

From September 1914

For those who remain standing on the battlefield

You who watch over earthly souls,
You who weave on earthly souls,
Spirits, you who protect human souls
Work lovingly out of cosmic wisdom:
Hear our plea, see our love
That would unite with your helping rays of strength
Devoted to spirit, sending love.

For those who have fallen on the battlefield

You who watch over the souls of the spheres,
You who weave the souls of the spheres,
Spirits, you who out of worlds' wisdom
Work lovingly, protecting soul humans:
Hear our plea, see our love
That would unite with your helping streams of strength.
Sensing spirit, streaming forth love.

From January 1918

IN MEMORY OF THOSE WHO HAVE DIED

May my love
Be sacrificially woven
Into all the protective sheaths
That surround you —
Cooling all warmth,
Warming all coldness —
Live carried by love,
Light-gifted, upward!

To Paula Stryczek
after the death of Anna Wagner
December 31, 1905

You to whom my love is streaming
May your warmth cool you
May your cold warm you
May my love's fidelity
See in the spirit
To your spirit future
Out of my heart forever.

Given to Rudolf Meyer
March 3, 1911

With you my soul seeks you,
Presciently divining,
Is with you
And lives your task
With you
So we are united
Karmically for all time.

To Gertrud and Wilhelm von Heydebrand
after the short life of one of their children
1911/12

Evenings:

May there be sent to you
My love just as it was
When you were here with me.
May it ease your heat
May it ease your cold,
So that you can find the way
From the soul- into the spirit-realm.

15-20 minutes

[Mornings:]

black red

As out of the black wood of the cross
Red roses of light spring forth
So out of the darknesses of the worlds
The brightness of the divine Sun springs forth
So out of good human hearts
Love's strengthening being springs forth,
May this take place in my soul.

(Peacefulness of soul)

Given to Matilda Björklöf
June 1913

Mornings:

In the primal beginning was the Word...

Midday:

May my love follow, follow you
Follow you in your pain
Follow you in joy.

Evenings:

The meditation as given in *An Outline of Esoteric Science* [CW 13, Rose Cross Meditation]*

To Anna Leuthel
on the death of her son
early 1915

[*See pp. 291-293 in *An Outline of Esoteric Science,* SteinerBooks/Anthroposophic Press 1997.]

Faithfully through the gates of death
I will follow your soul into the spirit's
Light-engendering time-places
Loving and easing Earth's coldness for you
Knowing, arranging spirit light for you
Thinking, I will stay with you
Reducing the worlds' searing heat.

To Gertrud Noss
on the death of her son Fritz Mitscher
February 1915

May my soul follow you into the spirit realm,
Follow you with the love
It was able to nurture in the earthly realm
When my eye could still see you,
May the heat and the cold be eased for you,
Thus we live united
Not separated by the gates of the spirit.

At the death of Gertrud Noss
September 1915

In the beginning was the Word
And I myself was in the Word,
And the Word was with God.
And with the Word I myself was with God.
And the Word was a God.
And a God beheld me in the Word,
And the Word should live in my soul.

Au commencement était le Verbe
Et dans le Verbe j'étais moi-même,
Et la Verbe était en Dieu.
Et avec le Verbe j'étais moi-même en Dieu,
Et un Dieu était le Verbe.
Et un Dieu me regarda dans le Verbe,
Et le Verbe doit vivre dans mon âme.

To Mr. Corré at the death of his father
Undatable

Drawing:

yellow star on a blue background

Just as the stars shine golden
Out of the blue background of the spirit
So out of the depths of my soul
Strong supportive forces shine.

To Hermine Stein
at the death of her son Friedrich
who fell in battle on March 22, 1915

Into the fields of spirit I will send
The faithful love we found
To bind soul to soul
Loving, you should find my thinking
If from the bright lands of spirit
Seeking, you turn your soul
To behold what you seek in me

Notebook, 1916

Making being
Giving light to *you* *To me*
In light's expanses
I am *You are*

At one in thinking-feeling
We strive
Interweaving
Soul in soul.

— Only in the realm of one's thoughts

— Should seek what it can give one in the form of experience of the spirit

Notebook, 1917

You were ours
And ours you will be
If the eye of your soul
Filled with devotion
Now radiates the light of the spirit.

Your thoughts'
Noble power will seek
In the worlds of the spirit
Our love, which we will
Faithfully preserve for you.

Notebook, 1917

May my love be the sheaths
That now surround you
Cooling your heat,
Warming your coldness
Sacrificially inwoven
Floating, carried by love,
Light-gifted, upward. —

Notebook, 1917

May our love follow you,
O soul, that lives there in the spirit,
That sees your life on Earth;
Seeing and knowing yourself as spirit.
And that which in soul land
Appears to you as your self, thinking,
May it accept our love
So that we may feel ourselves in you
And you may find in our souls
What lives with you in faithfulness.

On the death of Marie Hahn
September 1918

May heart-love reach to soul-love
Love's warmth stream to spirit's light
Thus I draw near to you
Thinking spiritual thoughts with you
Feeling cosmic love in you
Willing in spirit through you
Weaving unity of experience.

To Rudolf Hahn
for his wife Marie
September 1918

Evenings:

1.) *Rückschau* ["backward review" through the day]
2.) Imagining the world of the stars against a blue sky:

My I will be
In spirit-filled space
It will have left
Its body of flesh
It will weave
In the spirit of God
Filled with strength

Wait quietly
Think of him throughout the given meditation

Mornings:

Imagine the Sun
The Sun sounding tones in the heart:

Christ is with you
He fills your heart
Christ is in you
He fills your soul
Christ is around you
He fills your spirit
Feel him

Wait quietly

Imagine face

———

Imagine hands touch

———

Come, soul, to me
I am waiting
Come into my thoughts
They are waiting
Come into my feelings
They are waiting
My I is waiting.

To Theodora Cayley-Robinson
c. 1919/20

To you
In love
On the paths of Christ
Seek my heart
Live
In my thoughts
As I in your soul.

For a mother
after the death of her small child
June 1921

Into the sleep of your soul
Warming your heart
My thoughts stream.
Experience them in your liberated I.
I will be with you.
And I will bring you from earthly being
What you need for spirit-memory
Out of your earthly life.

To Margarete Bockholt
after the death of her father
January 1924

In the light of world thoughts
The soul weaves that
Unites with me on Earth.

Notebook , 1924

That the eyes of your soul may see
The deeper force in my thoughts
Thus is my will.
May my will meet your will
In the strength of the Father
In the mercy of Christ
In the light of the spirit.

To William Scott Pyle
following the death of Edith Maryon
May 1924

May my heart's warm life
Stream to your soul
To warm your cold
To alleviate your heat
In the worlds of the spirit
May my thoughts live in yours
And your thoughts in mine.

Notebook , 1924

1.) Es empfangen A Aa Ar im Aetherweben das
Schicksalsnetz des . . . .

2.) Es verweben in Ex. Dyn. Kyr. im Astralempfinden
des Kosmos die gerechten Folgen des
Erdenlebens des M. . . . . .

3.) Es auferstehen in Thr. Ch. Seraf. als deren Tatenwelten
die gerechtesten Ausgleichungen des
Erdenlebens des —

4. VII. 24

While writing on the blackboard Rudolf Steiner spoke these words: ... And as human beings we will be saying a beautiful, magnificent prayer when we think about the connection of life with death or think of someone who has died, and say the following:

1. May Angels, Archangels, and Archai receive in their etheric weaving the web of the destiny of ______ .*

2. May the just consequences of the earthly life of ______* be led before Exusiai, Dynamis, and Kyriotetes in the astral perception of the cosmos.

3. May the righteous forms of the earthly life of ______* be resurrected in Thrones, Cherubim, and Seraphim as the manifestation of their deeds.

Lecture, Dornach, July 4, 1924

*["those concerned."]

To lead you with strength
Into future earthly life,
You have been given to us
Through your parents' will.

In pain at death's door
Only soul-winged words
Destined for ripening life
Have the capacity to speak.

So instead of being prepared by school
For earthly deeds and life
Transport the loving memories
Of your teachers into that spiritual existence

Where the soul weaves around
The bright light of eternity
And the spirit experiences
The goal of the will of God.

Upon the death of a school child, Robert Kurzdörfer
May 1924

I look at you in the spiritual world
Where you are
May my love lessen the heat
May my love lessen the cold
May it reach you and help you
To find the way
Through the spirit's darkness
Into the spirit's light.

Undatable

May my soul's love strive toward you
May my love's understanding stream toward you.
May they carry you
May they hold you
In the heights of hope,
In the spheres of love.

Undatable

To you who linger in the realm of the spirit
May my love be your follower
May it follow you in your coldness
May it follow you in your heat
May it carry faithfully with you
What of your soul is to be carried
I with you.

Loose note sheet
Undatable

To you in spiritual being
May the warm power of love be born
The soul's best spiritual feeling
Living heat with you, soothing you
Bearing cold with you, strengthening you
And seeing you in me
And wanting me in you.

Loose note sheet
Undatable

May my love be with you in the spirit realm.
May your soul be found
By my seeking soul.
May your cold be lessened
And your heat be soothed
By my thinking of your being.
May we thus be bound together
I with you
And you with me.

Undatable

Into the worlds where lingers
Your soul's core
I send love to you —
To cool your heat,
To warm your cold.
And if you find me in feeling,
I will be forever close to you.

Undatable

So know, then, that your future vision of the spirit
Shall find constancy and loyalty in our souls,
Which we wish to hold for you continually
When loving-thinking we must seek you
In the realm of the soul through that gate,
Which shall reveal the power of the spirit
From us to you.

Loose note sheet
Undatable

Whatever happens to you
In the course of time and worlds
My loving heart
With all of its forces
Will be with you
Bearing
Helping.

Given to Lucie Bürg
Undatable

1. Your will was weak
2. Strengthen your will
3. I send you
   Warmth for your cold
4. I send you
   Light for your darkness
5. My love for you
6. My thought of you
7. Continue to become

To Franz Gerner
for a friend he lost to suicide
Undatable

Soul in soul land,
Seek Christ's mercy
That brings you help
Help from spirit lands
That grants peace even to those spirits
Who would despair
Lacking peace in earthly experience.

To a mother for her son
who took his own life

You my life's
Companion, help
Our son, my
Thoughts go
To you, rightly
To bring them
To him, I beg
Your soul, dear husband.

To this same mother, to seek help
from her husband, who died young
Undatable

FROM THE AFTER-DEATH EXPERIENCE

In the glowing,
There I feel
The life-force.
Death has wakened me
From sleep,
From the sleep of the spirit.

I will be,
And do those things out of myself
That the illuminating force
Streams forth within me.

The words of a young soldier who has died
Berlin, March 2, 1915

Into cosmic distances I will bear
My feeling heart, so that it becomes warm
In the fire of the holy forces working;

Into cosmic thoughts I will weave
My own thinking, so that it becomes clear
In the light of the eternal becoming of life;

Into depths of soul I will plunge
Devoted contemplation, so that it becomes strong
For the true goals of human activity;

In the peace of God I strive thus
With life's struggles and cares
Preparing myself for a higher self;

Aspiring to work in joyful peace,
Sensing world-existence in my own existence
I seek to fulfill my human duty;

May I then live in anticipation,
Oriented toward my destiny's star,
Which gives me my place in the spirit realm.

Address for Lina Grosheintz
January 10, 1915

Into human souls I will guide
Spirit-feeling, so that voluntarily
It may wake in hearts the Easter word;

With human spirits I will think
Soul-warmth, so that powerfully
They can feel the Risen One;

The earthly flame of spiritual knowledge
Brightly illumines the appearance of death;
The self becomes the eye and ear of the world.

For Lina Grosheintz
Notebook
Easter 1915

As soul, I am not on the Earth
But only in water, air, and fire;

In my fire I am in the planets
And in the Sun.

In my Sun-being I am in the
Fixed stars in the heavens —

As soul, I am not on the Earth
But in light, word, and life;

In my life I am within
The being of the Sun and the planets
In the spirit of wisdom.

In my wisdom-being
I am in the spirit of love —

Notebook
At the turn of the year 1917/18

I was united with you —
Remain united in me.
We will speak together
In the speech of eternal being.
We will be active
There, where deeds produce effects,
We will weave in the spirit,
There, where human thoughts are woven
In the Word of eternal thoughts.

Address for Georga Wiese
January 11, 1924

No barrier can separate
What united in the spirit
Preserves
The light-shining
Love-streaming
Eternal soul-bond
Thus I am in your memory
Thus are you in mine.

Draft

IN MEMORIAM

His soul rests in the Kingdom of Christ
The thoughts of his loved ones are with him.

Inscription for the gravestone of Johann Steiner
who died on January 22, 1910

Here she sought spirit-being
There may she find spirit-being
The thoughts of her loved ones
Remain with her.

Inscription for the gravestone of Helene Reebstein
who died on August 2, 1918

⊕

Im Leben war sein Sinnen
Dem Geiste zugewandt
So finde er im Tode
Des Geistes Leben.

Mit ihm sind
Seiner Lieben Gedanken.

⊕

In life his thinking
Was turned towards the spirit
May he find in death
The life of the spirit.

The thoughts of his loved ones
Are with him.

Inscription for the gravestone of Friedrich Stein
fallen in battle on March 22, 1915

To S. St.

You are irreplaceable to us
In our earthly ranks;
We are bound to you primordially
In the eternities of the spirit.

Dr. Rudolf Steiner

Memorial program for Sophie Stinde
December, 1915

Her thinking strove for the light,
Her heart worked from love.

Inscribed on the relief
modeled by Rudolf Steiner, of Sophie Stinde
died on November 17, 1915

II

Mantric Sayings for Anthroposophic Work

For buildings * for work groups and branches of the Society * for teachers, doctors, and priests

Signature of the Rosicrucian School

Ex Deo nascimur
In Christo morimur
Per Spiritum Sanctum reviviscimus

Munich, May 1907

From God I am born
In Christ I die
Through the Holy Spirit I am resurrected

Malsch, April 1909

From God's being the human soul arose
Dying, it can plunge into the ground of being
One day it will deliver the spirit from death

Munich, August 1911

From divinity humankind comes into existence
In Christ death becomes life
In the Spirit's world-thoughts the soul awakens

Dornach, January 1924

The four maxims of the Wisdom of the Pillars

J [achim]

In pure thought you find
The self that can support itself.

If you transform thought into image
You experience creating wisdom.

B[oaz]

If you condense feeling into light
You reveal the formative force.

Objectify the will into a being
And you create in world-being.

Munich Congress
May 1907

The Foundation Stone document for the Malsch Building

Your blessing
You great
Brothers
Who live in our thoughts
Who work in our feeling
Who pulse through our will
Who form what is below from what is above
Who spiritualize the below into the above
Our souls pray for your blessing
For the Malsch Theosophical Lodge.
Weave your life about the stone,
Which we here sink into the Earth, so that
What is thought, felt, and willed for this Lodge
May grow from the seed of your life.

Given and entrusted to the Earth
for the Malsch Lodge and its faithful guardians
and the Stockmeyer family in the presence
of the representatives of the theosophical Lodges
of Berlin, Dusseldorf, Munich, Stuttgart,
Nürnberg, Wiesbaden, Lugano, Karlsruhe,
Heidelberg, Bielefeld.
Dr. Rudolf Steiner

with approximately forty additional signatures

April 5, 1909

May there shine upon this building
The light of the spirits of the East;
May the spirits of the West
Reflect that light;
May the spirits of the North secure it
And the spirits of the South warm it through and through,
So that the spirits of the East, West,
North, and South stream through the building.

From the address at the laying of the Malsch Foundation Stone
April 5, 1909

Consecration of the Stuttgart Branch house

Spirit of the Universe, you who are the herald of our true self-knowledge, you have graciously kept the promise that you gave us, because you saw our work, as your servants have carried it out for many years. Today at this hour, it is made manifest. Truly, Great Spirit of the Universe, even the vastest spaces of the spirit cannot contain you, who penetrate all your works with your thoughts; you, who wish to dwell in the words that may sound from our lips. How much the less could these temple walls, which we have built, contain you. Spirit of the Universe, you who announce our real self-knowledge, behold the will to understand, the longing for knowledge among your servants! Look down upon us, Spirit of the Universe, who penetrates each I, and let your eyes be open over this building where you have decided to live! Hear our feelings, which impel us to show ourselves by means of our work to be worthy of the influence of your spirit in the rooms that we have dedicated to you!

Lecture, October 15, 1911

May whoever enters bring love to this home,
May whoever lingers here seek knowledge in this place,
May whoever departs take peace from this house.

Lecture, October 15, 1911

AUS MIR
VON JCH
JCH
JN ES
AN ES
DAS ES

Inscriptions on a sketch for the seven pillars for the large-domed room of the Johannes Building project

DAS ES	THE IT
AN ES	TO IT
IN ES	IN IT
ICH	I
VOM ICH	FROM THE I
AUS MIR	OUT OF ME
ICH INS ES	I INTO IT

Munich 1911/12

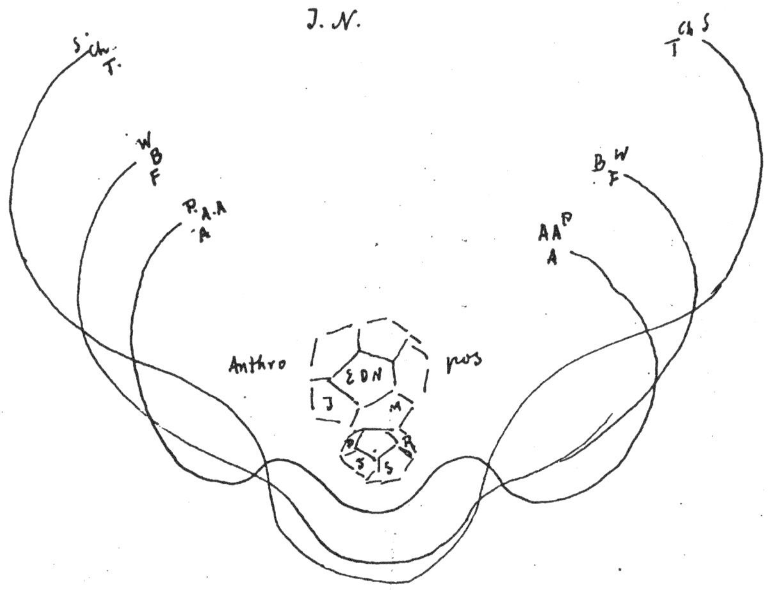

Als Eckstein unseres im Geist sich suchenden Willens, in der Weltenseele sich fühlenden Seins, im Welten-Ich sich ahnenden Menschen senken wir in der verdichteten

Elemente Reich

Dies Sinnbild der Kraft, nach der wir strebend uns bemühen durch

3 5 7 12

Gelegt ~~den 20 Tag des Monates September im~~ 1913 Jahre n. Chr. G. ~~d. i. 1880 Jahre n. d. M. v. G. da ☿ in der Waage als Abendstern stand.~~
vom Johannesbau-Verein für die Anthroposophische Arbeit am 20. 1. Tage des Septembermonats 1880 n. d. M. v. G. d. i. 1913 n. Chr. Geb. da ☿ als Abendstern in der Waage stand.

Transcription of the presentation for the Foundation Stone document for the Dornach building

In the name of

Seraphim
Cherubim
Thrones

Wisdoms
Movers
Shapers

Personalities
Archangels
Angels

Anthropos

Ex Deo Nascimur (From God we are born)
In... Morimur (In...we die)
Per Spiritum Sanctum Reviviscimus (Through the Holy Spirit we live again)

As the cornerstone
our will, seeking itself in the spirit,
our being, feeling itself in the world-soul,
human beings, intuiting themselves in the world-I
we sink into the condensed
Realm of the Elements
You, symbol of strength, for which striving
we seek by means of

3 5 7 12

Laid by the Johannes Building Society for Anthroposophic Work on the twentieth day of the month of September, 1880 years after the Mystery of Golgotha, 1913 years after the birth of Christ, as Mercury is the evening star in the constellation of Libra.

September 20, 1913

Draft of the macrocosmic Lord's Prayer

Amen

You who work through the worlds
    Wisdoms
    Movers
    Shapers
you had to send the evil
because of humanity's fall into the tempter's net
because he took existence and gave it to himself
therefore he needs daily bread
Because another will rules on Earth as in the heavens
And humanity separated itself from your realm
And forgot the name
Of the fathers in the heavens.

Draft, loose note sheet

The macrocosmic Lord's Prayer

Amen

Evils rule
Witnesses to selfhood separating itself
Selfhood-debt owed by others
Experienced in daily bread
In which the will of heaven does not rule
In which humanity separated itself from your kingdom
And forgot your name
You fathers in the heavens.

*From the address given at the laying of the Foundation Stone of the Dornach building, September 20, 1913**

*See pp. 334-340

Words on the window themes of the Goetheanum

I look
It reveals   It has revealed

West: Red

—

The world unfolds the will
The will gives birth to itself   It is born of the will

North: Green

—

The love of the world works
And human love arises   And human love grasps it

South: Green

—

The world gives him sight
And he sees   And he makes himself into a seeing being

North: Blue

—

The outer world making a decision
Deciding   He has willed

South: Blue

—

It has happened
It became It was

North: Purple

—

It arises
It will be It is

South: Purple

—

The world breathes piety
Thus he becomes pious The piety works

North: Rose Pink

—

The world builds
I see the building And the building becomes a human being

South: Rose Pink

Dornach, 1919/1920

For two sketches for the center themes of the green Goetheanum windows

And the spirit of gravity
Gathered the contradiction
And in the human will
It became
Resistance.

North

And the light
Of the spirits
Became the light
Of human beings.

South

1913/14

For the opening ceremony of the first event in the still unfinished [first] Goetheanum building

In the name of that spirit that announces itself
To the souls in our place of striving,
I appear in this moment
Before human beings who, from now on,
Want to hear the word
That rings out solemnly to the souls here.
In earlier times those powers that guide the goals
Of our earthly development
Could not yet manifest themselves
In a fully conscious way.
For as in children's bodies those forces
Destined to become the bearers of knowledge
Must gradually ripen and grow stronger,
So humanity as a whole must develop
During its earthly course.
Dull at first was the life of the soul's instincts
That later would prove themselves worthy
To behold the light of the spirit from high worlds.
But, in the Earth's beginning, higher powers of existence
Chose souls devoted to the spirit
As the wise leaders of humanity.
In the places where people strove for wisdom
These leaders cultivated the forces of the spirit
That sent into still only dimly conscious souls
Rays of knowledge with which
Souls could penetrate themselves by looking.

For the opening ceremony of the first Anthroposophical College Course

Only later could spiritual researchers
From the ranks of humankind draw students,
Who through a strong-willed life of testing
Proved themselves ripe in the brightness of consciousness
To strive single-mindedly for spiritual knowledge.
And as the students of the first leaders
Were later able to maintain the noble gift with dignity,
Unconscious leadership disappeared,
And free souls were able to strive consciously.
And these free souls then chose people,
Who would follow them in the care
Of the spiritual treasure; and thus it continued
From one human age to the next.
Until now, all places of true knowledge
have sprung legitimately from the highest,
Which stands in the spheres of the spirit.
Seeking earnestly, we strive here
For our true human spiritual inheritance.
We will never speak of knowledge
That does not bear the spirit's own seal
But speak only of the light from the spirit worlds
That contemplating human beings can develop for themselves
Who, striving, seek to entrust themselves to the light
In order to fathom the depths of their souls.
To stride worthily towards this light
Indicates the seriousness of this turn of an era
And its distress; the signs are in truth
Heavy with meaning, the signs that now reveal clearly
The eyes of the spirit in the world plan. —

Dornach, September 26, 1920

Closing words of the address at the opening ceremony of the first Anthroposophical College Course

To turn ourselves to the light
In the distress of dark times, —
May it be the will
Of the people here
At the dawn of the spirit
To send a glimpse of the soul —
And may it remain so forever and ever.

Lecture, Dornach, September 26, 1920

Spiritual Communion, draft

To think true human communion

There draw near to me in the working of the Earth
Given to me in the image of matter
The heavenly deeds of the stars
Which I wisely transform in feeling.

I experience myself with the world

The formative heavenly being of the stars
Penetrates me in the working of water
Grasping me in matter's powerful content
Which in willing I create with love.

I am with the world

Draft

Spiritual Communion

The heavenly beings of the stars
Coming close to me in the working of the Earth
Given to me in the image of matter
In willing I see lovingly transform themselves.

I experience myself as soul

The heavenly deeds of the stars
Penetrate into me in the life of water
Shaping me in the forceful power of matter
In feeling, I see them wisely transforming themselves

I experience myself as spirit.

For the lecture held in the Goetheanum
just before the outbreak of the fire,
Dornach, December 31, 1922

Feeling into one's breathing — gentle feeling

The power of the waves of the worlds surges within me
The will of the gods lives in the waves
Will of the gods, you fulfill me
I quicken you into human will
In human will, my being becomes
Forceful creative life
I work out of the I into the world.

Feeling into the circulation of the blood — gentle hearing

The power of human will quiets itself within me
May human thinking live in the quiet
Human thinking, you enlighten me;
I grasp you as God's thought
My archetypal being is in the thought of God
And archetypal being becomes light-creating in me
I think from God to the I.

Notebook, December 1922

After the Goetheanum fire

Thought was wound on thoughts
Creating joyfully the soul was spent
In forms sensation breathed
And so spirit and art united

Will you well explore the pain
In which fate has plunged us—
Feeling disappeared in smoke and flames
Joy in creation has found an end

The eye looks into rubble

Loose note sheet
1923

Es wollte im Sinnenstoffe
Das Goetheanum vom Ewigen
In Formen zum Auge sprechen
Die Flammen konnten den Stoff verzehren
Es soll die Anthroposophie
Aus Geistigem ihren Bau
Zur Seele sprechen lassen

Die Flammen Geister
Sie werden sie erhärten

In sensory matter
The Goetheanum from eternity
Sought to speak in forms to the eye
The flames were able to devour the material
Anthroposophy should let its building
Speak to the soul out of the spiritual realm
The flames of the spirit
Will support and strengthen it

Notebook, April 1923

See the Logos
In the scorching fire;
Find the solution
In the House of Diana.

Lecture, Dornach, December 2, 1923

*The ideal-spiritual laying of the Foundation Stone of the General Anthroposophical Society through Rudolf Steiner**

December 25, 1923, at 10:00 in the morning

Human soul!
You live in the limbs
That bear you through the world of space
Into spirit's ocean being:
Practice spirit remembering
In depths of soul
Where in presiding
World creator being
Your own I
Comes into being
In God's I
And you will truly live
In humankind's world being.

Human soul!
You live in the beat of heart and lung
That lead you through the rhythm of times
Into your own soul's feeling being:
Practice spirit contemplation
In soul equilibrium
Where the surging
Deeds of world becoming

*see note p. 359

Unite
Your own I
With the world's I
And you will truly feel
In human soul activity.

Human soul!
You live in the stilled head
That from the grounds of eternity
Discloses world thoughts to you:
Practice spirit beholding
In stillness of thought
Where the eternal goals of the gods
Grant the worlds' beings' light
To the individual I
To will freely
And you will truly think
Out of humankind's spiritual foundation.

At the turning point of times
The light of the world spirit
Entered the earthly stream of being;
Night-darkness
Had prevailed.
Day-bright light
Streamed into human souls;
Light,
That warms poor shepherds' hearts
Light,
That illumines
The wise heads of kings —

Divine light
Christ-Sun
Warm our hearts
Illumine our minds

So that what we found
From our hearts
What we guide
From our heads
Intentionally
May be good.

(Following the repetition of: Human soul! You live in the limbs ...)

For the Father-Spirit of the heights presides
In the world-depths begetting existence
Seraphim Cherubim Thrones
May what finds its echo in the depths
Ring forth from the heights:
Speaking:
Ex Deo nascimur.
The elemental spirits hear it
In the East, West, North, South
May human beings hear it.

(Following the repetition of: Human soul! You live in the beat of heart and lung...)

For the will of Christ presides around us
Blessing souls in the rhythms of the worlds
Kyriotetes Dynamis Exusiai
Let what forms in the West
Be enflamed by the East:
Speaking:
In Christo morimur.
May human beings ...

(Following the repetition of: Human soul! You live in the still head...)

For the spirit's world thoughts preside
In light-imploring world being
Archai Archangeloi Angeloi
Let what is heard in the heights:
Be asked for from the depths:
Speaking:
Per Spiritum Sanctum reviviscimus.
May human beings ...

Lecture, Dornach, December 25, 1923

Second version

printed in "What is taking place in the Anthroposophical Society. News for Members," Nr. 1, January 13, 1924

Human soul!
You live in the limbs
That bear you through the world of space
Into spirit's ocean being:
Practice spirit's remembering
In depths of soul,
Where in presiding
World creator being
Your own I
Comes into being
In God's I;
And you will truly live
In humankind's world being.

For the Father-Spirit of the heights presides
In the world-depths begetting existence:
You spirits of forces
May what finds its echo in the depths,
Ring forth out of the heights,
Speaking:
Humanity's being is from the divine.
The spirits of the East, West, North, South hear this:
May human beings hear it.

Human soul!
You live in the beat of heart and lung
That leads you through the rhythm of times
Into your own soul's feeling being:
Practice spirit contemplation
In equilibrium of soul,
Where the surging
Deeds of world becoming
Unite
Your own I
With the world's I;
And you will truly feel
In human soul activity.

For the will of Christ presides around us
Blessing souls in the rhythms of the worlds:
You spirits of light
Let what forms in the West
Be enflamed by the East:
Speaking:
In the Christ, life becomes death.
The spirits hear this in the East, West, North, South:
May human beings hear it.

Human soul!
You live in the stilled head
That from the grounds of eternity
Discloses world thoughts:
Practice spirit beholding
In stillness of thought,
Where the eternal goals of the gods
Grant world's beings' light
To the individual I
To will freely;
And you will truly think
Out of humankind's spiritual foundation.

For the spirit's world-thoughts preside
In light-imploring world being.
You spirits of the soul
Let what is heard in the heights,
Be asked for from the depths:
Speaking:
In the spirit's world thoughts the soul awakens.
The spirits hear this in the East, West, North, and South:
May human beings hear it.

At the turning point of times
The light of the world spirit
Entered the earthly stream of being;
Night-darkness
Had prevailed;
Day-bright light
Streamed into human souls;
Light,
That warms poor shepherds' hearts;
Light
That illumines
The wise heads of kings —

Divine light
Christ-Sun
Warm our hearts;
Illumine our minds;

So that we found
From our hearts
What we lead
From our minds
Intentionally
May become good.

January 1924

Haus „Friedwart"

Friede walt' in diesem Haus;
Das bedenk' ein jedermann,
Der da gehet ein und aus,
Herzhaft stark, so viel er kann.

Friedwart House

May peace preside in this house;
May those who go in and out of it
Keep this in mind
With strength of heart, as they are able.

Administrative Building, Dornach
Spring 1920

The laying of the Foundation Stone for the Vreede House

May soul live in this house
May it be permeated with spirit
Seeking firm will
In the depths
So that devout consciousness
May develop
In every room of the building
And so that from above
The blessings of the spirit
And the grace of God
May be able to unite
In all who live within.

The foundation stone was sunk into the Earth on the twenty-seventh of October, 1921. Those who participated in the arising of this building give this stone to it, their thoughts reflecting what is written above.

Arlesheim, October 27, 1921

Verse for the Foundation Stone for the renovation of the Free Waldorf School in Stuttgart

May that rule, which brings the strength of the spirit in love
May that work, which brings the light of the spirit in goodness
Out of the heart's certainty
Out of the soul's constancy
To the young human being
For strength in the work of the body
For the innerness of the soul
For the brightness of the spirit.

To this may this place be consecrated:
May youthful minds find in it
Guardians of what is human
Endowed with strength, devoted to the light.

In their hearts remembering the spirit
That should preside here,
Those who as a symbol
Sink this stone
To make firm the foundation
Of lives, sovereignty, and action:

Liberating wisdom
Strengthening the power of the spirit
Revealing the life of the spirit.

This they wish to declare
In Christ's name
With pure intentions
With good will. —

42 signatures

December 16, 1921

For the school in Hamburg-Wandsbeck

Out of the seriousness of the time
Must be born
The courage to act.

Give to your teaching
What the spirit gives to you,
And you will free humankind
From the nightmare
That burdens you
Through materialism.

1922

For the Christian Rosenkreutz Branch in Nice

Great exalted spirit
You who fill the vastness of the worlds
Who dip into the soul's foundations
Fill our place of work
Fill our seeking souls
Strengthen our will
Warm our feeling
Purify our thinking
Now and evermore.

1911

For the Consecration of the Novalis Branch in Rome

Spiriti eccelsi, che eravate perfetti
Prima che scorresse la sorgente del nostro principio,
La vostra Sapienza Creatrice formo l'universo,
E dal mondo della Vostra Sapienza sorse:

La Forza del nostro pensare
La Vita del nostro sentire
Il Fine del nostro volere.

Che la Vostra Forza, la Vostra Vita, il Vostro Fine
Cpmpenetrino gli organi delle anime nostre:
Onde possano contemplare la Vostra Sapienza Creatrice,
Onde possano vivere il Sentire Creativo,
Onde possano creare nel Volere Divino.

Ex Deo nascimur
In Christo morimur
Per Spiritum Sanctum reviviscimus

⊕

High Spirits, you who were complete
Before the wellspring of our beginning began to flow,
Your creating wisdom formed the world,
And from your world of wisdom emerged

The strength of our thinking,
The life of our feeling,
The goal of our willing.

May your strength, your life, your goal
Pour themselves into our souls' members,
So that they may behold our creating wisdom,
So that they may live your creating feeling,
So that they may create in godly willing.

Ex Deo nascimur
In Christo morimur
Per Spiritum Sanctum reviviscimus

April 1910

For the meetings of the Novalis Branch in Rome

Nel segno della croce
Circondata da rose
Vediamo sentendolo
Il risveglio dello Spirito del Mondo
dalle profonditá dell' anima
Le forze nascoste del mistero.
Forze che agivano nel principio,
Forze che devono agire alla fine,
Forze nelle quali
    noi oensando siamo,
    nelle quali
    noi amando viviamo,
    nelle quali
    la devozione respiriamo.

In the sign of the cross
By roses surrounded
Feeling, we see
The world spirit awakening
From the soul's depths.
May the mystery of hidden forces
Be released from the soul depths.
Forces, which worked in the beginning,
Forces, which should work at the end,
Forces, in which
    We are when we think,
    In which
    We love and live,
    In which
    We breathe reverence.

To be said at the beginning and the end of each gathering in such a way that each time a different member says this verse aloud, while the others fill themselves with its content meditatively. Once every member has had a turn, the first person begins the cycle again.

c. 1911

For the Emerson Branch in London

Out of the light-filled heights of the spirit
May God's bright light shine
In human souls
Who wish to seek
The grace of the spirit
The power of the spirit
The being of the spirit.

May it live
In hearts
Inwardly in souls
Ours
We feel ourselves
Gathered here
In His name. —

On the opening of the first members' meeting
1913

For the founding of the St. Michel Group in Paris

Great encompassing spirit
May my thinking raise itself
To your wisdom
May my feeling raise itself
To your revelation
May my willing raise itself
To your creative work
Thus may my soul
Sense you three ways
And unite itself in its depths
With your being
  Now
And in all time.

May 1913

For the consecration of the Vidar Branch in Bochum

> You, who guide spiritual life and give human beings what they need according to their epoch, work together with our friends here in this city, when filled with devotion they serve the spiritual life.

We wish to send this as a prayer to the spiritual leaders, the higher hierarchies in this moment, which is solemn in a twofold way....

That this may serve as our Christmas prayer today: also, that this Branch may become a living witness of what flows as a force from the higher worlds into human development and is increasingly able to give to human souls the consciousness of the truth of these words:

In the vastness of space
Things speak to the senses,
Changing in the stream of time;
Recognizing this, the human soul,
Not limited by the vastness of space
And untouched by the flow of time,
Penetrates into the realm of eternities.

Lecture, December 21, 1913

For the founding of the Mannheim Branch II

To experience in the soul's interior
What, as the essential kernel of the human being,
Binds us eternally to the world spirit
And so gives true meaning
To life and striving:
This is what penetrates the science of the spirit.
And may this also preside among and over us,
So that we may become one for the work of the soul;
May life's great spirit guides
Grant us their grace and love,
Blessing us in this work.

In commemoration
of the Society for Spiritual Science
Being formed in Mannheim
December 21, 1915 Rudolf Steiner

December 1915

Verse for the consecration of a room in Tannbach Castle

You yourself — knowing, feeling, willing human —
You are the riddle of the world
What it hides
Is revealed in you, becoming
Light in your spirit,
Warmth in your soul,
And the strength of your breathing
It binds for you bodily wisdom
To the world of the soul
To the realm of the spirit.
It leads you into matter
So that you can see yourself as human
It leads you into spirit
So that you do not lose yourself spiritually.

For Ludwig and Bertha von Polzer-Hoditz
June 10, 1918

For the work group of Alice Kinkel in Stuttgart

The sphere of the spirit is the soul's home;
Human beings reach there,
If they take the way of true thinking,
Choose the heart's power of love
As their strong leader,
Opening their soul's inner sense
To the script that, revealing itself
Everywhere in the being of the world,
They can discover each time
As a proclamation of the spirit
In all that lives and acts,
And also in all things,
Spread out lifelessly through space,
And in all that happens
In time's stream of becoming.

Rudolf Steiner

1923

For the founding of the Threefold Group in New York

May our feeling penetrate
To our heart's midpoint
And seek to unite itself in love
With the human beings working toward the same goal
With the spirits who, full of grace, look down
Upon our seriously heart-centered striving
Strengthening us from regions of light
And illuminating our love.

November 1923

To the Friends in Berlin

Human beings see
With a world-begotten eye;
What they see binds them
To the joy and pain of the world;
It binds them to all that unfolds there,
But binds them no less to all that plunges
Into the abyss of the realm of darkness.

Human beings see
With an eye bestowed by the spirit;
What they see binds them
To the spirit's power of hope and support;
It binds them to all
That is rooted in eternity
And that bears fruit in eternity.

But human beings can see
Only if they themselves feel the inner eye
As an organ of the spirit of God
That in the theater of the soul
In the temple of the human body
Performs the deeds of the gods.

Humankind is
Oblivious of God's inner nature,
But we wish to take it
Into the bright light of consciousness
And over the rubble and ashes
Bear the flame of the gods into human hearts.
May lightning bolts shatter
Our sensory houses into rubble;
We shall build soul houses
Out of the knowledge
Of light's weaving, strong as iron.
And the sinking of the outer
Shall become the rising
Of the soul's innermost depths.

Pain presses close
From the power of matter's force;
Hope shines,
Even when darkness cloaks us;
And one day after the darkness
When we are allowed to live in the light again
Hope will press into our memory.
When one day the light comes,
We do not want to miss this illumination
Because in our present pain
We did not plant hope in our souls.

November 1923

Consecration verse for the branch room of the Berlin youth

Protecting us, the walls of our room separate us
From the disturbing din and bustle of the world;
In stillness, the soul finds its way
To the soul in spiritual space;
What the strongest wall holds apart,
World forces bind effectively together;
Thus, forcefully love must bear
Human forces into the soul's union with spirit.

Easter 1924

Protecting us, the walls of our room separate us
From the disturbing din and bustle of the world;
In stillness, the soul finds its way
To the soul in the unbounded spirit region
But world forces weave in the cosmos
What the strongest wall holds apart
Thus, forcefully love must bear
Human forces into the soul's union with spirit.

Draft

For the teachers of the Free Waldorf School

In the gleam of sense being
Lives the will of the spirit,
Giving itself as the light of wisdom
And concealing inner strength;

In one's own being's I
May human will gleam
As thinking's revelation,
Self-supporting on its own forces;

And may one's own force
Powerfully unite the light
Of world wisdom with the self:

Shape me, so that I may
Turn myself to the divine heights
Seeking the forces of illumination.

September 1919

For the teachers of the Free Waldorf School

Spiritual sight,
Turn yourself seeing within;
Heartfelt feeling-touching
Stir the soul's delicate being;
In prescient spirit sight,
In heart-natured feeling-touching,
There conscious being weaves.
Conscious being from the higher
And the lower parts of human nature
Binds the worlds' brightness
To Earth's darkness.

Spiritual sight
Heartfelt feeling-touching
Behold, taste
In the human interior
Worlds' brightness weaving
In Earth's prevailing darkness:
My own
Human-formative-force
Generating
Force-creating
Will-bearing —
My Self.

October 17, 1923

From the last letter to the teachers of the Free Waldorf School

May the activity of thought unite us,
Since we must be separated in space. —
May what we have already achieved together
Now be put into action by the community of teachers.
May its range increase through your own counsel,
Since that counselor, who would so gladly come,
Does not have his wings free to do so.

Goetheanum, March 15, 1925

For anthroposophical doctors

Preparation: Where do I find the good?

1. Can I think the good?

I cannot think the good.
Thinking supports [takes care of] my etheric body.
My etheric body works in my body's fluidity [liquidity].
Thus I shall not find the good in the body's fluidity.

2. Can I feel the good?

I can certainly feel the good, but is not there through me, if I only feel it.
Feeling supports my astral body.
My astral body works in my body's aeriform element.
Therefore, I do not find the good that exists through me in my body's aeriform part.

3. Can I will the good?

I can will the good.
Willing supports my I.
My I works in the warmth ether of my body.
Therefore in the warmth I can realize the good physically.

I feel my humanity in my warmth.

1. I feel light in my warmth.

(Take care that that this sensation of light arises in the region of the physical heart.)

2. I feel the substance of the world resonating in my warmth.

(Take care that this specific sensation of sound moves from the lower body to the head, then expands throughout the whole body.)

3. In my head, I feel the life of the world stirring in my warmth.

(Take care that this specific sensation of life spreads from the head throughout the whole body.)

To Helene von Grunelius for the physicians
Fall 1923

What I am now writing on blackboard is not so that you will know it, but rather so that it may repeatedly arouse in you this quickening of your medical consciousness. Something like:

You healing spirits
You unite yourselves
With Sulphur's blessing
Of the etheric fragrance;

You quicken yourselves
In the ascent of Mercury
To the dewdrops
Of what grows
And becomes.

You come to a halt
In the Salt of the Earth
That nourishes
The root in the ground. —

This is, so to speak, what the soul acquires by observing everything around it, awakening the inner sense for what surrounds it. The human being may then answer:

I will unite my soul's knowing
To the fire
Of the blossoms' aroma;

I will arouse my soul's life
With the glistening drops
On the morning leaves;

I will strengthen my soul's being
On the hardening salt
With which the Earth
Attentively cares for the roots. —

Lecture, Dornach, January 5, 1924

Experience the fire You change with the being of the Sun.	Warmth ♄
Experience the air You change with the light of the Sun.	Light ☉
Experience the water You change with the working of the Sun.	Chem. ☾
Experience the Earth You change with the life of the Sun.	♂ ☿

Notebook
January 1924

In signs human beings think
        In the bones

In image-change human beings see
        In the muscles

In shaping tone human beings feel
        In the organs

In meaningful word human beings will
        In the activity of the organs.

Notebook
For the lecture on January 7, 1924

You are soul
The body is God's
Being in you

May the spirit
Dwell within your soul
May the spirit
Dwell within your body

May you allow the divine Godhead
To preside in the spirit of the body
And allow the I
To preside in the spirit of the soul

Because if the spirit of your soul
Takes your body for itself as strength
Then you are sick in body
And if your soul takes the spirit of your body
For itself as strength
Then you are sick in soul.

Notebook
January 1924

Behold in your soul
    Force of illumination
Feel in your body
    Power of heaviness

In the force of illumination
    The spirit-I radiates
In the power of heaviness
    The spirit of God is at work

But the force of illumination
    May not grasp
The power of heaviness
    Nor the power of heaviness
Penetrate
    The force of illumination

Then if the force of illumination grasps
    The power of heaviness
And if the power of heaviness penetrates
    Into the force of illumination
Then in the madness of the world
    Body and soul
Will bind themselves
    Together in corruption. —

Lecture, Dornach, January 9, 1924

At the threshold there stream into one another
Sensory darkness and spirit brightness
And become deception

The image of this deception
Is illness

The guardian lives in this illness.
The encounter in the spirit is conscious
The encounter in the body is unconscious.

Notebook
January 1924

In ancient times
There lived forcefully in initiates' souls
The thought that each human being
Was sick by nature.
And education was seen
As equivalent to the process
Of healing, which would at the same time
Bring about with the child's maturity
The health needed for the perfection of human-being.

In the first newsletter for physicians
March 11, 1924

Behold what happens cosmically,
And you will sense the human form. ☾

Behold what moves airily,
And you will experience the ensouling of the human being. ☉

See what changes earthily
And you will grasp the inspiriting of the human being. ♄

Lecture, Dornach, April 22, 1924

Feel in the fever's measure
Saturn's spiritual gift

Feel in the pulse's count
The Sun's soul force

Feel in matter's weight
The Moon's forming power:

And then you will see in your will to heal
The earthly human being's need for healing.

Lecture, Dornach, April 24, 1924

Move the child's early years
Into its old age
And the child's old age
Into its youth:
And the human etheric being
Will appear to you
Condensed
Behind the being of the body.

Move the density of old age
Into the time of human maturing
And the age of maturity
Into the life of youth:
And you will hear
The working of the human soul
Resounding in cosmic tones
From the etheric life.

Lecture, Dornach, April 25, 1924

Feel thinking!

It has lost:
The burdens of the Earth
The weaving of the air
The shining of the cosmos

Strengthen thinking!

It will gain:
The burdens of the Earth just a little
The weaving of the air to a greater extent
The shining of the cosmos to the fullness of life

Feel willing!

It has lost:
The working of the cosmos
The speaking of the air
The thinking of the Earth

Strengthen willing!

You shall gain:
The working of the cosmos quite distinctly
The speaking of the winds almost understandably
The Earth's sensing softly living

Loose note sheet
April 1924

From ancient, holy sacrificial sites
The healing art once flowed
Into the works of humankind

Remember your revelation:
Say it at the new healing site.
And if human souls
Carried by the spirit
Hear your call to the Mysteries
Then they shall work
To bring forth healing
In the weaving of human life.

I will seek the power of spirit-ears
In a loving heart
To hear the call.

Draft

Mercury-Raphael spoke

I) Observe the old practice:

At the worthy holy site
Formations of flame grasp hidden earthly powers,
Bearing them in Mercury's seal, the fiery snake,
Toward the gods —
That in healers may act
What in the depths of the chasms
In the blowing of the winds
In the streaming of the lights
Wards off Earth evils. —

II) Renew the old practice:

Tell what is reborn
At the new healing site
Through your striving:
If human souls
Carried by the spirit
Hear thinking
About the newly-ignited fiery snake-seal
And wish to work to bring forth healing
In the life-weaving of humankind.
May they praise you:

I will arouse spirit-ears-power
In the loving heart
To hear your healing-word. —

For the inner circle of physicians
September 1924

May there dwell in hearts
In the illuminating brightness
Of human beings
A helper mind.

May there work in hearts
In the warming power
Of human beings
Helper strength.

Work in the hearts
Of human beings
In warming power,

So let us bear
The full will of the soul
In the warmth of the heart
And in the light of the heart,

Thus may we bring
Healing
To those in need of healing
Through God's sense of mercy.

For nurses, 1924/25

To live in the spirit,
In soul being
Finding oneself, weaving:
The self acts,
And in the Sun's heights
Truly carries the human being
To world-creator-power.

For Paul Klein, priest
1914/15

Im Gefühle der Bedürftigkeit DEINER Gnade,
Christus-Licht der Welt, harre ich
nach Kräften
öffnend der Seele Pforten
DEINER Erleuchtung
Still in mir will ich sein
und DIR danken DEINER Gabe
und sie geben
als DEIN Geschenk an Menschen
Werkzeug DEINES Wortes
will ich sein
mit meiner Seele
besten Kräften
echten Tiefen
stillsten Ehrfürchten.

In feelings of the need for YOUR mercy,
Christ-light of the world, I hope for and await
          forces
          opening the portals of the soul
     For YOUR illumination
   I will be still within myself
   and thank YOU for YOUR gift
   and give it
   as YOUR gift to humankind
   An instrument of YOUR word
   will I be
with my soul's
          best powers
          true depths
          stillest reverences.

Loose note sheet

To YOU
Bearer of the Worlds' Word
may my soul
be directed
opening itself to YOUR
portal of grace,
to YOUR
gate of love;
Send the spirit,
who bears
YOUR Word's
illumination
YOUR Word's
warmth of love
YOUR Word's
heart power
Into my soul.

May stillness reign within me
May stillness weave through me
That I may hear
The voice of YOUR spirit
The wise guidance of YOUR spirit
That out of me
may speak
What YOU deem worthy
To place in the depths
of my heart.
Keep watch on my word
Keep watch on my thinking
Keep watch on YOUR servant
And YOUR messenger.

For Pastor Paul Klein
as a meditation before delivering a sermon
August 1911

Consciousness fills me,
That I must be a temple
Of the World-Creator-Word.

May my eye learn to see in darkness
May my mouth learn to speak in silent stillness
May my heart learn to feel in spirit-purity:

I see Sun-spirit in Moon-soul,
I speak God's Word in earthly ears
I feel spirit-streaming in human blood.

For female priests of the Christian Community
1923

I will walk the path
That releases the elements in events
And leads me down to the Father
Who sends illness to balance karma
And leads me up to the spirit
Who guides the soul in its errors
To the acquisition of freedom
Christ leads downward and upward
Harmoniously creating a spiritual human in an earthly human.

For doctors and priests, Dornach
September 18, 1924

III

Free Translations of Biblical Texts

FROM THE OLD TESTAMENT

The Beginning of Genesis

B'reschit bara elohim et
haschamajim w'eth ha'arez.

In what was created the gods created
that which reveals itself
and that which moves itself in itself
What moves itself in itself was
disordered and darkness.

Notebook, 1910

In the primal beginning the gods conceived what reveals itself and what produces itself in itself —
And what produces itself in itself was in itself confused and desolate and darkness lay over the desolation and the breath of the gods brooded about what reveals itself.

The gods spoke — let it become light; and it became light
And the gods saw that the light was beautiful and they made a division between the light and the darkness
And the gods named the light day and the darkness they named night.
Then the dark and the breaking-through of light became a day.

Notebook, 1910

In what had come over from Saturn, Sun, and Moon existences, the gods conceived in cosmic activity what reveals itself outwardly and what moves itself inwardly.

And over what moves itself internally, and through what moves itself, deep darkness ruled. But it expanded from there inward, and brooded there over the darkness, penetrating it with warmth, the creative spirit of *Elohim — Ruach.*

Lecture, Bern, September 4, 1910

The Ten Commandments

Second Book of Moses, Chapter 20

I.

I am the Eternal-Divine that you sense within you. I have led you out of the land of Egypt, where you could not follow me inwardly. From now on, you should not place other gods above me. You should not recognize as higher gods what an image shows you of anything appearing in the Heavens above, or from the Earth, or acting between Heaven and Earth. You should not worship anything that is lower than the Divine within you. I am the eternal within you, and I am a continuing Divinity. If you do not recognize me within you, I will disappear as the divinity in your children, grandchildren, and great-grandchildren, and their bodies will decay. But if you recognize me within you, I will live on into the thousandth generation as you, and the bodies of your people will thrive and prosper.

II.

You should not speak in error of me within you, because every error regarding the I within you will corrupt your body.

III.

You should separate workdays from feast days, so that your existence becomes an image of my existence. Because what lives as the I within you formed the world in six days, and lived in itself on the seventh day. Therefore your actions, and the actions of your son, and the actions of your daughter, and the actions of your servants, and the actions of your livestock, and the actions of all who are with you, should be turned outward for only six days; but on the seventh day your gaze should be turned inwards to seek me in you.

IV.

Continue to work as your father and mother worked, so that possessions that they gain by dint of their efforts, which I formed within them, remain your property.

V.

Do not murder.

VI.

Do not break marriage.

VII.

Do not steal.

VIII.

Do not reduce the worth of your fellow human beings by saying untruths about them.

IX.

Do not look enviously on what your fellow human being owns as property.

X.

Do not look enviously at the wife of your fellow human being, nor at his servants and other beings by means of which he progresses through life.

Loose note sheet
Berlin, November 16, 1908

FROM THE NEW TESTAMENT

The Gospel of Matthew, Chapter 5

The Beatitudes of the Sermon on the Mount

Blessed are the beggars for the spirit, for theirs is the kingdom of heaven.

Blessed are the gentle, for within themselves they shall receive the Earth as their share.

Blessed are the mourners, for they shall find comfort within themselves.

Blessed are those who hunger and thirst for justice, for they shall be satisfied within themselves.

Blessed are the compassionate, for to them through themselves compassion will be shown.

Blessed are the pure in heart, for they shall behold God within themselves.

Blessed are those who bring about peace, for they shall be called the children of God.

Blessed are those who are persecuted for the sake of justice, for the kingdom of heaven shall be within them.

Asked by the Pharisees, when the kingdom of God would come, he answered them and spoke: The kingdom of God comes with a perception; it shall not be said that it is here or it is there, for see: the kingdom of God is among you.

First version, 1905

1. Filled with God are those who are beggars for the spirit, for in they themselves is the kingdom of heaven.

2. Filled with God are those from whom affliction is not lifted (who are subject to suffering), for they will seek aid for themselves through themselves.

3. Filled with God are those who bridle their passions, for the Earth shall be given to them as their lot.

4. Filled with God are those who experience hunger and thirst for justice, for they shall be satisfied through themselves.

5. Filled with God are those who love, for they shall awaken love.

6. Filled with God are those who are pure in heart, for they shall see God within themselves.

7. Filled with God are those who bring peace, for they shall be called sons of God.

Second version, 1910

The Gospel of Mark, Chapter 8

And Jesus left, and his disciples accompanied him to places around Caesarea Philippi. And as they went their way, he spoke to those who were around him: What do the people say about what the I might be? What do people acknowledge as the I? —

Thereupon those who were around Jesus answered him, saying: People say that John the Baptist must live in the I if the I is truly to be. But others also say that this I must be permeated with Elias, and Elias must live in the I; still others say, another of the prophets must be involved, so that the I says: Not I, but the prophet within me is acting. —

But he spoke to those who were around him: What do you say, then, is the I? — Then Peter answered: The I must be grasped so that we cognize it in its spirituality as You, that is, as the Christ! —

And then he answered those who were around him: Beware of saying this to ordinary people! For they cannot yet understand this secret. —

To those around him, however, who were inspired by his words, he began to teach the following: That, in human beings, what outwardly and physically expresses I-ness must suffer a great deal if this I-ness in human beings is to revive fully. And just as it once was, it must agree with the oldest masters of humanity and those who know what lives in the holiest wisdom and say: In the form in which it is present, it cannot be used; this form must be killed, and following the rhythm determined by earthly circumstances, it must be brought to life again in three days out of a higher form. —

And they were all dismayed, as he spoke these words freely and openly.

> [Here I must make a comment. Until this moment, it had been permitted for one to speak words of this kind only in the Mysteries. It was a secret that had been spoken only within the Temple of the Mysteries up until this point: the secret that a human being had to pass through the "Die and Become" in initiation and had to wake after three days. This explains the following passage, which reads:]

Peter was stunned, and took Christ aside and told him that such a thing could not be said freely and openly. Then Christ Jesus turned to him and said:

If you say such a thing, Peter, then it was put into your mind by Satan; for the way you speak of this truth, which lies before our time, belongs to the past; then it had to be confined to the Temple. In the future, this truth regarding the primal mystery of Golgotha will be able gradually to become known to all of humankind. The divine guidance of earthly development has determined it thus. And whoever speaks otherwise does not speak out of divine wisdom, but changes divine wisdom into the temporal form it had for human beings in the past.

Lecture, Berlin, March 7, 1911

The Beginning of the Gospel of John

In the primal beginning was the Word, and the Word was with God, and a God was the Word.

This was in the primal beginning with God.

All became through the same, and other than through this nothing of what arose became.

Among these was life, and life was the light of human beings.

And the light shone into the darkness, but the darkness did not grasp the light.

There was a person, he was sent from God, with his name of John.

This man came as a witness, so that he could bear witness to the light, and that through him, all should believe.

He was not the light, but a witness to the light.

For the true light, which illumines all human beings, was to come into the world.

It was in the world, and through it the world became, but the world did not cognize it.

It came to individual, single human beings (it reached I-human beings); but the individual, single human beings (the I-human beings) did not receive it.

But those who received it could reveal themselves through it as children of God.

Those who trusted His name did not become through blood, or the will of the flesh, nor of human will, but through God.

And the word became flesh and lived among us, and we have heard his teaching, the teaching of the only Son of the Father, filled with devotion and truth.

John bore witness for him and clearly announced: This was the one of whom I spoke, of whom I said: After me, one will come, who was before me. He is my predecessor.

From his fullness we have all taken grace upon grace.

For the law was given through Moses, but mercy and truth is through Jesus Christ.

Until now no one has seen God with his eyes. The only-begotten Son, who was in the World Father, has become the leader in this seeing.

Lectures, 1904/1908

Interpretation of the Christ-Impulse through the Michael-Impulse

First Millennium:

In the primal beginning was the Word,
And the word became flesh
And dwelled among us.

Second Millennium:

And human flesh must again become thoroughly filled with spirit,
So that it is capable of living in the realm of the Word,
In order to behold the divine secrets.

Lecture, Dornach, November 22, 1919

In the primal beginning was the Word,
And the Word was with God,
And a god was the Word.
This was in the primal beginning with God.
It was there, where all came to be,
And nothing came to be
Except through the word.
Life was in the Word,
And life was
The light of human beings.

Lecture, Pforzheim, March 7, 1914

In the beginning is the thought,
And the thought is with God,
And the thought is a divine thought.
In it is life,
And that life should become the light of my I.
And may the divine thought shine into my I,
So that the darkness of my I may grasp
The divine thought.

Lecture, Pforzheim, March 7, 1914

In the beginning is the thought,
And the thought is an infinite one,
And the life of the thought is the light of the I.
May the illuminating thought
Fill the darkness of my I,
So that the darkness of my I may grasp the thought,
The living thought,
And live and weave in its divine primal beginning.

Lecture, Pforzheim, March 7, 1914

In the beginning is memory,
And memory lives on,
And memory is divine.
And memory is life,
And this life is the human I
That streams through human beings themselves.
Not they alone, but the Christ in them.
When they remember divine life,
Christ is in their memory,
And as a radiant, shining memory-life
Christ will shine light
Into every immediately present darkness.

Lecture, Pforzheim, March 7, 1914

In the primal beginning was the force of memory.
The force of memory should become divine,
And something divine should become the force of memory.
All that arises in the I
Should become t h u s :
That it is something that has arisen
Out of enchristed, divinely penetrated memory.
In it should be life,
And in it should be the streaming light
That out of self-recalling thinking
Shines into the darkness of the present.
And may the darkness, just as it is present,
Grasp the light of what has become divine.

Lecture, Pforzheim, March 7, 1914

The Gospel of John, Chapter 17

The High Priestly Prayer

Jesus placed himself in spiritual vision and spoke:
Fatherly Ground of the World:
let the work of your Son be revealed,
so that through the work of your Son
You will also be revealed.

You have made him the creative one
in all fleshly human bodies,
that he may lead all into the future alive,
who came to him through you.

They will live in the future because
their soul's eye is prepared
to see you as the one true ground of the world
and of the work of Christ Jesus,
whom you have sent to them.

Through me you were revealed again in earthly existence,
when the Earth shrouded your revelation.
Such was your will that worked through me.

So, too, fatherly Ground of the World,
now let stream forth the revelation,
that through me already had become,
before you were revealed in the earthly world. —

Through me the Word became
that revealed you, manifested in human souls
who came to me through you.
You were in them,
through you they came to me,
and they took into themselves
Knowledge of you.

They recognized that
what I spoke to them
was spoken to them
by you through me.

Fatherly Ground of the World, this I beseech,
that those who have come to you through me,
may always live with you,
as I am with you,
and that they may see there your revelation,
that you lovingly let radiate before me,
before yet the Earth was.

Through me was revealed the Word
that revealed you
and I will bear this Word into human souls,
so that the love, with which you love me,
may be preserved in them,
and also that my eternal life
may be eternally preserved in their lives.

Lecture, Dornach, September 21, 1922

Letter of Paul to the Corinthians, Chapter 13

In Praise of Love

But I show you the way that is higher than all others:

If I could speak out of the spirit with the tongues of human beings or of angels, and lacked love, my speech would be sounding brass and a ringing bell.

And if I could prophesy and reveal all secrets, and communicate all the knowledge of the world, and if I had all faith that could move the mountains themselves, and yet lacked love, it would all be nothing.

And if I were to distribute all the spiritual gifts, even if I gave my body to be burned, and yet lacked love, it would all be to no purpose.

Love endures forever. Love is benevolent, love does not know envy or jealousy, love does not know bragging, does not know pride, love does not injure what is worthy of respect, love does not seek its advantage, does not let itself be provoked, does not hold bad deeds against someone, does not rejoice in injustice, is delighted only by truth.

Love clothes all, streams through all belief, may hope for everything, and may practice tolerance everywhere.

If it is love, it can never be lost. What one prophesies passes away when it is fulfilled; what one speaks with tongues ceases when it can no longer speak to human hearts; what is known, ceases when the object of knowledge is exhausted.

For all knowledge is a patchwork and incomplete, and all prophecy is a patchwork and incomplete.

But when completion comes, the incomplete, the patchwork is left behind.

When I was a child, I spoke as a child, felt and thought as a child; when I became an adult, the world of the child was over.

Now we see only dark outlines in the mirror; but one day we shall see the spirit face to face. Now my knowledge is an incomplete patchwork; but one day I shall fully cognize how I myself am.

Belief is enduring, hope in security is enduring, love is enduring; the greatest among these is love; therefore love stands at the very top.

Lecture, Cologne, January 1, 1913

The Letter of Paul to Timothy, Chapter 3

The mystery of the way of God can be known.
He who revealed himself in the flesh,
But whose being is in itself spiritual,
Who is fully recognizable only to the angels,
But who can still be preached to the heathen,
Who has life in the belief of the world,
He is raised into the sphere of the spirits of wisdom.

Esoteric Lesson, Cologne
May 9, 1912

The Esoteric (Apostles') Lord's Prayer

Father, you were, are, and shall be in all our innermost being!

Your being is in all of us exalted and highly praised.

May your realm expand in our deeds and in our life changes.

May we carry out your will in the conducting of our lives as you, O Father, have placed it in our innermost mind and soul.

You offer us the food of the spirit, the bread of life, in superabundance in the changing circumstances of our lives.

Let there be compensation in our compassion for others for the sins committed against our beings.

You do not allow the tempter to act in us beyond the capability of our strength, because in your being no temptation can exist; because the tempter is only appearance and delusion, from which you, O Father, shall safely lead us through the light of your insight.

May your power and glory act within us in the courses of time of the courses of time.

Before 1913

The Lord's Prayer in the Wulfila Bible

Atta unsar thu in himinam,
Weihnai namo thein.
Qimai thiudinassus theins.
Wairthai wilja theins, swe in himina jah ana airthai.
Hlaif unsarana thana sinteinan, gif uns himma daga.
Jah aflet uns thatei skulans sijaima, swaswe jah weis
  afletam thaim skulam unsaraim.
Jah ni briggais uns in fraistubnajai,
ak lausei uns af thamma ubilin;
Unte theina is thiudangardi jah mahts jah wulthus
    in aiwins. Amen.

...If we try to translate this wonderful prayer of the ancient Goths into the language of today, we may not translate word for word, but must say something like:

We sense you up there in the spiritual heights,
All-Father of humankind.

Hallowed be your name.

May the realm of your dominion come to us.

May your will rule as so in heaven,
so also on Earth.

All-Father, whose name forms the outer corporeality of the spirit, whose realm of dominion we wish to acknowledge, whose will should reign, You,

You should also penetrate the earthly
so that daily we shall see our bodies arise anew
in a certain sense through earthly nourishment.

So that in our social lives we do not become the debtors
one of one another, so that we stand over against one another
As equal human beings, so that we do not decline
With the bodily-spiritual:

Let us not decline into that which out of our bodies
brings our spirit into darkness,
But deliver us from the evils
that arise when we decline too strongly
with our spirit into our bodily being.

Yours is the claim to dominion,
Yours is the right to power,
Yours is the revelation as light, as radiance,
As all-powerful social love.

Lecture, Dornach, May 15, 1921

THE MACROCOSMIC LORD'S PRAYER

Address at the Laying of the Foundation Stone of the Dornach Building

September 20, 1913

My dear sisters and brothers,

Today, on this festive evening, let us truly understand one another. Let us understand that for the soul this deed signifies, in a certain sense, a solemn vow or pledge. Our striving has brought it about that here, in this place, from which we can see far out into the four elemental directions of the compass rose, we are allowed to erect this emblem of the spiritual life of the modern age. Let us understand that, insofar as we feel our souls united with what we have laid symbolically into the Earth, we have today committed ourselves to the spiritual stream of the evolution of humankind that we recognize to be right and true.

Let us try, my dear sisters and brothers, to make this solemn promise in our souls: that in this moment we will look away from all of the small concerns of life, from all that must necessarily bind us, as human beings, with everyday life. In this moment, let us awaken within ourselves the thought of the bond between the human soul and the striving at this turn of an era. Let us try to think for a moment on the fact that, since we have done what we wished to accomplish this evening, we must carry within ourselves the consciousness of looking out into far, far cycles of time, to become aware of how this mission, whose emblem this building is intended to be, fits into the great mission of humankind upon our earthly planet. Let us try, not with pride or presumption, but with humility, devotion, and a willing sense of self-sacrifice, to direct our souls upward toward the great plans and goals of human activity on the Earth. Let us try to place ourselves in the state in which we ought actually to be; and in which we must be if we are to understand this moment correctly.

Let us try to think how the great tidings and message, the primeval, eternal gospel of divine-spiritual life, long ago passed into earthly evolution, and how it passed over the Earth in the days when the divine spirits themselves were still the great teachers of humankind. Let us try to place ourselves, my dear sisters and brothers, back into those sacred ages of the Earth, of which a last yearning and memory rises up in us when we think of ourselves in ancient Greece, surrounded by the last echoes of mystery wisdom and the first tones of philosophy; hearing the great Plato telling of the eternal ideas and the eternal *hyle* ("matter") of the world. And let us try to grasp what since those times has spread across earthly evolution as luciferic and ahrimanic influences. Let us try to make clear to ourselves how our connection with divine world existence, with willing, feeling, and divine-spiritual cognition, has disappeared.

In this moment, let us try, deep, deep down in our souls, to sympathize with what human souls feel in the countries of the East, North, West, and South; souls whom we may recognize as the best ones, who do not get beyond what we can express with the words "an undefined longing and hoping for the spirit." Look around you, my dear sisters and brothers, and see how this undefined longing and vague hope for the spirit prevails in humanity today! Feel and listen, here by the Foundation Stone of our emblem and landmark, how the cry for an answer may be heard in the vague longing and hoping of humanity for the spirit; for an answer that can be given only where spiritual science is able to preside with its gospel of knowledge of the spirit. Try to inscribe into your souls the greatness of this moment that we are experiencing this evening.

If we could hear humanity's yearning call for the spirit and wanted to erect the true Building of Truth from which the message will be proclaimed more and more; if we can feel this in the life of the world, then this evening truly we will understand one another. Then, neither in pride nor in the overestimation of our striving, but in humility, in devotion and willingness for self-sacrifice, we will know that in our effortful striving we must be the ones who continue the spiritual work that has been lost in the Western world in the course of the advancing evolution of humanity. This development, however, had to lead through the countercurrent of ahrimanic forces to the point where humanity stands today. Now, if the longing cry for the spirit is not heard, the soul will wither and waste away. Dear sisters and brothers, experience these anxieties! We must do so, if we are to be allowed to continue to fight that great spiritual battle, which is a battle glowing with the fire of love in the great spiritual battle that must continue, and which was once led by our ancestors when they repelled the ahrimanic onslaught of the Moors.

Led by karma, we stand at this moment in a place through which important spiritual currents have passed. Let us feel within ourselves this evening the full seriousness of the situation. Long ago humanity reached the final point in its striving for personality. When, in the fullness of this earthly personality, the heritage of the divine leaders of the primeval beginning of earthly evolution had withered away, the Cosmic Word appeared in the East:

In the beginning was the Word

And the Word was with God

And the Word was a God.

And the Word appeared to and spoke to human souls: fill earthly evolution with the meaning of the Earth! Now the Word itself has passed over into the aura of the Earth and has been received by the Earth's spiritual aura.

Four times the Cosmic Word has been proclaimed through the centuries, which will soon amount to two millennia. Thus has the light of the world radiated into earthly evolution.

Ever deeper Ahriman sank, and had to sink. Let us feel ourselves surrounded by human souls in which resounds a longing cry for the spirit. But let us feel too, my dear sisters and brothers, how these human souls must continue their universal cry of longing because Ahriman, dark Ahriman, is spreading chaos over the spiritual knowledge of the world of the higher hierarchies. Feel that the possibility is present to add to the Word of the spirit, already proclaimed four times, another proclamation that I can present to you only in a symbol.

From the East came the Light and the Word of the proclamation. From the East it moved West, proclaimed four times in the four gospels, waiting and expecting the coming of a mirror from the West, one that would add knowledge to what is still only a proclamation, spoken four times, of the Cosmic Word. It goes deeply into our hearts and souls when we take in that Sermon, spoken there on the Mount when the period for the maturing of the human personality was fulfilled and the ancient light of the spirit had faded away, and the new light of the spirit had appeared. The new light of the spirit had appeared!

And after it appeared, it moved from East to West through centuries of human development, waiting for understanding of the words that once resonated into human hearts in the Sermon on the Mount. Out of the depths of world evolution, as the Mystery of Golgotha was consummated, resounded that first, eternal prayer, spoken as the proclamation of the Cosmic Word. That immemorial prayer resonated deeply. It was to make known to the microcosm the mystery of existence in the depths of the soul, and out of the innermost reaches of the human heart. It was to be heard ringing out from East to West, what we know as the "Lord's Prayer." But this Cosmic Word itself contained, waiting, as it sank into the microcosm in those earlier days, what would sound forth one day in the fifth gospel. Human souls would first have to mature further in order to understand what is most ancient from the Western point of view, because the macrocosmic gospel was meant to sound like an echo resonating in the microcosmic gospel of the East.

If we are able to bring understanding to the present moment, then an understanding can open within us for the idea that a fifth gospel can be added to the four extant gospels. May these words, which express the secrets of the macrocosm, resound this evening in addition to the secrets of the microcosm.

As the first aspect of the fifth gospel shall here resound the macrocosmic counterimage of the microcosmic prayer, which was first proclaimed from the East to the West. May the macrocosmic world prayer reverberate as a sign of our understanding and appreciation. It is contained in the fifth, ancient, and original gospel, which is connected with the Moon and with Jupiter, as the four gospels are connected with the Earth.

AUM. Amen.
Evils reign
Witness of I-ness, separating itself,
Guilt of selfhood incurred through others,
Experienced in the daily bread
In which the will of heaven does not reign
Because human beings separated from your kingdom
And forgot your names,
You Fathers in the Heavens.

The Lord's Prayer was given as the prayer of humankind. The microcosmic Lord's Prayer, which was proclaimed from the East to the West, now sounds forth toward the ancient macrocosmic prayer. It resounds thus if it is properly understood, when it sounds its way out into the vast spaces of the worlds and is echoed back with the words shaped by the macrocosm. Let us take the macrocosmic Lord's Prayer with us, feeling that with this prayer we are beginning to gain an understanding for the gospel of knowledge: the Fifth Gospel.

From this important moment, let us carry home in our souls with the seriousness and dignity of our will the certainty that all wisdom sought by the human soul—if the seeking is genuine—is a countercurrent of cosmic wisdom, and that all human love that is rooted in the selfless love of the soul is fructified by the love that presides in human evolution.

Through all earthly periods and in all human souls a strengthening through cosmic force works out of the strong human will, which finds fulfillment in the sense of existence and the sense of the Earth. Today, humankind begs for this cosmic force, turning its attention uncertainly toward a spirit it hopes to find, but is unwilling to recognize, because Ahriman has sunk unconscious fear into the human soul whenever spirit is spoken of. In this moment, let us feel this, my sisters and brothers. If you feel this, you will be able to arm yourselves for your spiritual work; to "prove yourselves" as human beings who manifest the light of the spirit through the power of thought, even when dark Ahriman seeks to spread the darkness of chaos over the fully awakened clairvoyant capacity, dulling wisdom. Fill your souls, sisters and brothers, with the longing for true knowledge of the spirit, in accordance with true human love and a strong desire. Try to awaken within yourselves the spirit who can trust the language of the Cosmic Word, which echoes back to us out of the vast reaches of the universe and of space, sounding its way into our souls. That is what one must truly feel this evening, if one has grasped the meaning of existence: human souls have reached the limit of their striving. Feel what should happen with this symbol, this landmark, whose foundation stone we have laid today; but feel this with humility, not with pride; with devotion and willingness to sacrifice, not with hubris. Feel the meaning of the knowledge that we should gain because we are able to know this: that the veil enveloping the spiritual beings in the vast reaches of space must be broken through in our time if spiritual beings are to speak to us of the meaning of existence.

Human souls everywhere around us will need to take in the meaning of existence. Hear how in different spiritual places spiritual science, religion, and art are spoken of, and take action accordingly; hear how much more empty the soul forces of striving have become. Feel that you must learn to fructify these soul forces by means of spiritual imagination, inspiration, and intuition. Feel what can be found if you correctly hear the tone of creative spirituality.

Those who in addition to the ancient Lord's Prayer can learn to understand the meaning of the prayer of the Fifth Gospel will be able to recognize and thoroughly understand this meaning and purpose in and for our time.

When we learn to understand the sense of these words, we shall seek to take up and nourish the seeds that must bloom if earthly evolution is to continue and flourish, rather than withering. Through human will, the Earth can reach its goal, which has been determined from the earliest reaches of time.

Feel this evening, then, that wisdom and the meaning of the new knowledge, the new love, and a new strong force must become alive in the souls of human beings. Souls that will blossom and bear fruit in future earthly evolutions will need to understand what we are assimilating into our souls for the first time today: the macrocosmically reverberating voice of the ancient eternal prayer.

AUM. Amen.
Evils reign
Witness of I-ness, separating itself,
Guilt of selfhood incurred through others,
Experienced in the daily bread
In which the will of heaven does not reign
Because human beings separated from your kingdom
And forgot your names,
You Fathers in the Heavens.

Thus we take our leave from one another, taking with us in our souls a consciousness of the meaning and importance of the seriousness and dignity of the deed that we have carried out. The consciousness of this evening should spark within us the striving for knowledge of a new revelation given to humankind. The human soul thirsts for this, and shall drink from it; but not until it shall fearlessly win belief and trust in what spiritual science can proclaim. And spiritual science, for its part, should unite what for a time was separated in human evolution: religion, art, and science. Let us take this idea with us, my sisters and brothers, as a memory of this communally celebrated hour that we do not ever wish to forget.

(Then followed the covering and cementing of the foundation stone).

EDITORIAL AND REFERENCE NOTES

Page 4; and 5, "Through the power of thinking..."; "In exceptional being, discover..."

These two notes are next to each other and clearly belong together in Notebook 427. However, in Notebook 427 above the note *In exceptional being...* is written "Motzkus." Both of these notes may well have been written down in connection with H. P. Blavatsky's *Secret Doctrine*, which Rudolf Steiner interpreted for Theosophists in Berlin in 1903. See also the section "The Seven Great Life-Secrets and the Masters" in CW 264, pp. 215-222, in *From the History and Contents of the First Section of the Esoteric School 1904–1914*. The drawing, however, is to be found only on a loose note sheet, note 575, and not in the notebook. The following fragment is found on two pages that come before this:

The virtues of Manas that have been raised to a spiritual level

Justice: Brotherhood
Restraint: Enthusiasm
Constancy: Pathos
Cleverness: Harmony
Symbolism: Sacrifice
Free piety: Reverence in freedom, Blessedness
Wisdom: Inspiration

If spiritual power streams into your virtues, they transform your knowing into loving:

If your thinking makes you just in your dealings with your neighbors, your loving thinking makes you empathetic and compassionate with your brothers:

If your thinking gives you moderation with regard to desire and aversion, loving thinking will give you enthusiasm for your spiritual wishes and desires:

If your thinking stays steadfast in the floods of the state of exceptional being, so too your loving thinking ....(fragment ends here)

Page 11, "The force of blossoming..."

A preliminary version of this in the same notebook reads as follows:
The power to germinate unites itself with the light and lives
The driving force unites itself with wisdom and loves.

Page 12, "Father... Word... Spirit..."

A photostat of this (with comments) is found in *Beiträge* #67/68, 1979. See also Berlin, November 10, 1904, in *Beiträge* #78, 1982/83.

Page 15, "Self in spirit"
According to Marie Steiner's Notebook 13, this is "for Johanna Mücke."

Page 24, "In the darkness I find the existence of God"
In the notebook with this stands also: "Know – I / Darkness – God"

Page 31, "Michael! Lend me your sword"
The German original is no longer available. The wording is a translation back into German from an Italian translation made at that time.

Page 42, "Cube of salt"
This saying, along with the following two, are next to each other in Notebook 450: I glimpse the plant... and I place before me the image of a lion...

Page 45, "It thinks me: Piety"
For the abbreviations *E.d.n. i....m. P.s.s.r.* see also page 239:

From God we are born
In Christ we die
Through the Holy Spirit we live again

For the mark "—" see also the Esoteric Lesson, Cologne, January 2, 1913, in CW 266/III: "...This is the reason why the esotericist is silent in word and thought at the point where the Holy Name, not meant to be spoken, would have to be named."

Page 55, "From above in Ja..."
Nothing further is known about the sequences of sounds IA [written JA] and MEB [which the translator believes most likely represents *Mein eigenes Bewußtsein*—"my own consciousness"]. In the draft in Notebook B 413, the first three lines read: From above in *Ia* [*Ja*]/From the front in *aum*/From the left in *MEB*," whereby the three lines may only have had the three sounds *aum*. Then the *a* was expanded to *Iao* or *Jao*, although the *o* was crossed out again; the *u* was expanded into *aum* and the *m* into *meB* or *MEB*.

Page 55, "Force lives "
In the original document, the words "hovering" and "guardian spirit" were written in shorthand; the transcription of "hovering" is not legible.

Pages 56-57, "In luminous heights"
Marie Steiner published the draft of this verse for the first time in 1929 in the *Nachrichtenblatt* [*News Bulletin*] #14. In 1935, she placed it in the volume *Wahrspruchworte – Richtspruchworte*, with the title "Sommer" ["Summer"] and the remark "out of a notebook." Most likely she knew nothing specific about the verse. In later editions the verse is not included, but it is placed in GA 261 (see *Our Dead*, CW 261) instead, because there are notes about life after death in that section of the notebook.

Just recently this final version (p. 57) became accessible from a sheet of paper found in the archives of the Ita Wegman estate. The page carries the tiny annotation "5/III.1915" [March 5, 1915], presumably in the handwriting of the unknown recipient. This evidence makes it seem unlikely that this verse was intended as a commemoration of someone who had died. This is confirmed by the lovely neologism "*Libillen.*" (In the draft this was thought to be a typo and "corrected" to read "dragonflies" (*Libellen*).

Page 59, "O you powers"
In the lectures, Steiner said the following about this: "What I have just said to you, my dear friends, is not simply an invented prayer. Instead, after Christ had experienced the Mystery of Golgotha, this is how he taught certain people to pray, those who were still able to understand him at the time when he remained with his close followers [students] after overcoming death through the Mystery of Golgotha."

Page 63, "Victorious spirit"
Marie Steiner gave this the designation "Meditations to take hold of the will" upon its first publication in *Aus den Inhalten der Esoterischen Schule* [*From the Contents of the Esoteric School*], Vol. 2, Dornach 1948. In another transcript it is called "Asking for Strength"; and in yet another the next-to-last line reads: "Rules/ prevails as the source" [*waltet* rather than *wallt*].

Page 64, "Ahriman, you are"
This verse is found in GA 197 [*Contradictions in the Development of Humankind*] next to notes for the lecture in Stuttgart, November 14, 1920.

Page 74, "Light floods"
In the notebook, the three verses stand one after the next between notes for the lectures held in May 1923, in Oslo:

Light floods the vastness of space...

If I dive deeply into the power of thought...

To pass by in the sea of being....

The abbreviation "Esot." is above them, and thus they were probably part of the esoteric lesson given on May 18, 1923, in Oslo.

Page 76, "I gaze into the universe"
Apparently this is closely connected to the essays "On the Life of the Soul" in the weekly circular *Goetheanum* of October/November, 1923 (reprinted in GA 36, "Thoughts on the Goetheanum"). Nothing more specific is known about how this verse came to be written.

Page 84, "I take you"
HIERAO, Greek *hieromai* = to be a priest, from *hieros* = holy, connected with the gods. The numbers refer to lotus flowers.

Page 88, "Ever-shining"
Both of these verses are found together in the notebook, so perhaps they belong together. They stand between notes for the lectures held on October 7 and 12, 1923, in GA 229. See in English, *The Four Seasons and the Archangels,* Rudolf Steiner Press, London 2002.

Page 92, "I can know"
Simone Rihouët-Coroze communicated that she met Rudolf Steiner when he was

giving lectures in Paris in May, 1924. He asked her how things were going for her. When she answered that she thought she could no longer continue her work on the French periodical *Science Spirituelle* because she lacked the inner strength to do so, he took a notepad from his pocket and wrote her this verse.

Page 97, "In you the human essence lives"
The meaning of the upper-case and lower-case letters in the left margin is unknown (A, B, e, G, i, D, o, H, u, V, Z; see facsimile on p. 96). It is possible that the Greek letters alpha, beta, gamma, delta, eta, epsilon, and zeta are meant here.

Page 107, "Fire forces of the Seraphim"
The following draft is found in Notebook 618:

"Forces of fire seraphic
Powers of imagery cherubic
Carrying the forces of the throne
Suns in the vastness of the worlds
Spirits in . . ." [incomplete]

Page 108, "To feel oneself in the head"
The following is found directly above this verse, separated from the rest of the page by a long line:

"⊕
To glimpse in the sign
That which at the Earth's beginning"

This is probably an unfinished draft.

Page 130, "Presiding in peace"
A draft on the same page reads as follows:

First day: Reigning peace illuminate my will through my thinking

O Creator of the Universe

Second day: Giving love, my will sacrifices

Page 140, "Light around me"
From a letter written to Rudolf Steiner by Professor Krüger: "Lübeck, November 8, 1911—Esteemed Dr. Steiner! You will hardly remember at this point that I asked you for some friendly advice on July 19th this year. I wanted to learn how to master my thoughts, since I am so nervous. You recommended at that time that I spend a suitable amount of time reading German poems, or something similar, backward [from the end to the beginning]. I was instructed to report on the success of this method a few months later, and that you would be so kind as to give me further suggestions. I did these exercises regularly. I ran out of German poems rather soon, so I conjugated irregular Greek verbs backward, and recited tables of historical dates backward. The success of this was clear: and I am extraordinarily thankful to you, esteemed Dr. Steiner, for your friendly advice. To

be sure, the success is still in its early stages, but I am already able to move away from those thoughts, which dominated and depressed me in the past. Would you please be so good as to give my brother-in-law or sister-in-law (handing you this letter) a further behavioral guideline or a new exercise, which s/he will then report to me?..."

Page 144, "In my heart I find strength"
This was written for Felicitas Stückgold to recite every evening in order to stabilize her health. See: Elisabeth Steffen, *Selbstgewähltes Schicksal [Self-Chosen Fate]*, Vol. 2, p. 185.

Page 155, "Think of the inside of your head"
The two following meditations were written for the same patient.

Page 157, "What life from its depths"
W.J. Stein reports that he received this meditation during a very difficult time in his life. (See: Johannes Tautz, *Walter Johannes Stein—A Biography,* Temple Lodge Press, London 1990 [*Eine Biographie*, Dornach 1989, Appendix, p. 261].

Page 157, "Quiet calm spreads"
Given to W.J. Stein following a shattering experience on March 9, 1924. Following this, Rudolf Steiner wrote him an undated letter: "My dear Dr. Stein! Experiences such as yours must be accepted internally in a purely objective way, without any agitation, as if one were merely observing the event. You should have the feeling that whatever is going to happen will take place only when one observes the experience in complete calm and quiet. Then such experiences do not take hold of the body, but weave themselves into the spirit, instead. That is essential. The fact that you have come to this point is a good result of the lively way you have given yourself over to concrete ideas from the spiritual world. Now you must accept, with utter serenity, that the ideas carry their spirit-soul aspects into the experience of the spiritual. Observe: 1. Quiet calm spreads itself../There can be no inner turmoil or tumultuous thoughts in your soul. Emotions darken the spiritual and draw strength from the physical. My most heartfelt thoughts [are with you] Rudolf Steiner." (See also J. Tautz, *Walter Johannes Stein—A Biography* [*Eine Biographie*, Dornach 1989, p. 109f.])

Page 159, "My head bears"
During Rudolf Steiner's stay in Stuttgart for a pedagogical conference, April 8-11, 1924, he gave this to W.J. Stein personally, also in connection with the experience of March 9, 1924. (See also J. Tautz, *Walter Johannes Stein—A Biography* [*Eine Biographie,* Dornach 1989, p. 113])

Page 161, "The stars are shining"
This was written on a receipt from the Clinical-Therapeutic Institute, Stuttgart, 88 Gänseheide Street, where the consultation for this patient took place. The recipient published the sheet as a facsimile in the *Mitteilungen aus der Anthroposophischen Arbeit in Deutschland [Communications/Announcements from the Anthroposophical Work in Germany]*, #131, Easter, 1980. The last line is *next to* the previous line in the original, most likely due to a lack of space.

Page 164, "Le soir"
From the French original, with minor corrections.

Page 167, "May there descend"
Another copy of this has the word "power of spirit [*Geistesmacht*]" in place of "force of spirit [*Geisteskraft*]."

Page 186, "You, spirit of my earthly space"
In the lecture on September 30, 1914, as well, this spirit is designated as a spirit of the people [*Volksgeist*].

Page 187, "From the mercy-bestowing soul of the world"
Helene Röchling (whose maiden name was Lanz) supervised and guided the war hospital built in the Heinrich Lanz Hospital in Mannheim, which was endowed by her family. See *Contributions* [*Beiträge*] #120, 1998.

Page 189, "I will believe"
The sheet of paper (#6612) from the hand of Rudolf Steiner comes to us from the estate of Helen Röchling. She was a close friend of Eliza von Moltke, from whose estate we have the copy (#6612a). The wording of this sheet is identical to the entry in Notebook 100. From this we must conclude that both women asked for a helpful meditation for Helmuth von Moltke, who was Chief of Staff at the beginning of World War I. The content tells us that the verse was not given to Moltke himself.

Page 192, "Spirits of your souls"
Rudolf Steiner spoke these memorial words, or similar ones, before every lecture given to members of the Anthroposophical Society during WW I in the countries affected by the war.

In Note 7164 for Alfred Zeissig in Vienna and in Notebook 104, Rudolf Steiner explicitly gives the singular and plural variations: "Spirits of your [singular] soul, active watcher,
May your [singular] efforts bring
Supplicating love to my soul..."

and corresponding changes were made to the other lines. This is also discussed in the lecture on January 19, 1915, in GA 157. In English, see *The Destinies of Individuals and of Nations,* Anthroposophic Press, New York 1986.

Page 195, "May my love /"
Rudolf Steiner wrote about this in his letter to Paula Stryczek at the death of Günther Wagner's wife: "It is important that you have the correct feelings when you say the words 'warmth' and 'coldness.' We are not speaking of the physical warmth or coldness, but rather about the warmth and coldness of feeling, although the human being in a physical hull [wrapper] has trouble forming an image of what these characteristics mean for those who no longer have bodies. First they must become aware that the astral body is still effective, even though it cannot make use of physical tools, or means. Much of what the human being strives for on Earth is given to him via physical means. Now these are no longer available.

This lack of physical organs is similar to—but only *similar* to, not identical to—the feeling of burning thirst, carried over into the realm of the soul. These are the strong 'sensations of heat' following the loss of the body. Much the same is true of the desires of the will. The will is used to making use of physical organs, and now no longer has them. This sense of 'deprivation' is similar to a feeling of cold within the soul. Living human beings are able to step in and provide help with regard to these feelings in particular, because these feelings are not the results or consequences of an individual life, but are bound together with the mystery of incarnation. For this reason, it is possible to come to the aid of those who have lost their bodies."

Page 196, "You to whom my love is streaming"
In the original version, due to an error, the third line reads: "May my [rather than *your*] cold warm you."

Page 197, "As out of the black wood of the cross"
A mistake may have crept into the last line as it was being copied, and perhaps it should have read:

"May this take place in *your* [rather than *my*] soul."

Page 205, "May our love follow you"
This was given to Pastor Hugo Schuster as a prayer for the burial service for Marie Hahn.

Page 209, "That the eyes of your soul may see"
This was requested by W. Scott Pyle following the death of Edith Maryon. Both of them were in the governing body of the Goetheanum Branch.

Page 211, "May the just consequences of the earthly life of ___ be led before…"
In his lecture, Rudolf Steiner said, "When we say *verwesen*, we mean "to lead before" [not "to decay," which would be the usual meaning of the word]. With this in mind, we construct the sentence: "May the just consequences of the earthly life of ___ be led before…."

Page 216, "So know, then"
In Note 3411, the last two lines read: "In the realm of the soul, through the gate of the spirit / May it open to allow us to reach you."

Page 218, "Soul in soul land"
The draft in Note 7211 reads as follows:

"Soul in the land of the soul,
Seek the mercy of Christ
That brings you help
Help for such souls
Who find peace only with difficulty"

Page 219, "In the glowing"
In Rudolf Steiner's lecture on March 2, 1915, before these words were spoken: "I can thus tell you about just such a young deceased person, who passed through

the portal of death at a young age, using words which have, may I say, broken through: words which seem surprising to some extent because they prove how the person who has died can find a way into this entirely different experience of life after death. He experienced death with particular clarity because he died on the battlefield. We see how he works his way out of his perceptions of earthly life and into new perceptions about life in the spiritual world. I would like to share these words with you, as well. It is as if they had been intercepted—if I may characterize them in this way—as they were being spoken by someone who had died on the battlefield, to those he had left behind. In the glowing...."

Page 220, "Into cosmic distances I will bear"
and p. 221. *Into human souls I will guide...* The text as printed here is that of the final version (Memorial Letter for Lina Grosheintz [Gedenkblatt für Lina Grosheintz]). At the speech given at her cremation on January 10, 1915, the first verse was spoken twice. The first time, at the beginning of the speech, the last two lines were spoken as follows: "Oriented toward my destiny's star, which gives me my place in the spirit realm." The second time, at the end of the speech, these lines were spoken thus: "Headed for my *stream* of destiny, which will *show me the stars* in the realm of the spirit." Rudolf Steiner pointed this out in Note 6512.

Here is a very brief excerpt from the lecture given on June 17, 1915, on the origin of the two verses:

> "Some time ago, in Dornach, we saw a member leave the physical plane after a relatively long life. Now you know that one who steps through the portal of death first leaves behind the physical body. For a time one continues to carry the etheric body, and then one must also lay aside the etheric body. And then comes a time when human beings must work to achieve a consciousness that will be their own between death and a new birth. Immediately after death, one occupies one's etheric body ... Now this was outside of the physical body, in the etheric world, which was shaped by what she had taken in concerning spiritual science, so that it became the expression of the soul of the person concerned. A few days later, at the cremation of the person concerned, it was necessary for me to say precisely these words, which I had perceived directly out of this person's soul. The words belonged to her, that is, not to me. I needed to say these words at the cremation: 'I want to bear my feeling heart into the vastness of the worlds...' Then the time came, which more or less everyone must pass through after death, metaphorically (and incorrectly) known as the time of sleeping, because when one has shed the etheric body, one has actually very much entered into the spiritual world. One is part of it.... And thus it happened that we were able to observe how this soul came to achieve this orienting consciousness by participating in our meetings—truly, while participating in our meetings. This participation was distinctly felt at our Easter celebration in Dornach this year... That was a completion, I'd like to call it, of what happened immediately after her death. It is the same soul that spoke the words (which I just read: "I want to bear my feeling heart...") immediately after her death, when she was still in her etheric body, which—as a result of her participation in this Easter lecture—was then able to say: 'I want to guide the spirit-feeling into human souls...'"

Page 231, "Signature of the Rosicrucian School"
This is the designation that Rudolf Steiner used for the words *"Ex Deo nascimur..."* in his lecture on May 21, 1907, at the Munich Congress held on Pentecost 1907... See *Rosicrucianism Renewed,* CW 284. Given officially by Rudolf Steiner for the first time at this event. The wording itself is much older, however. It appears in the Rosicrucian text "Fama Fraternitatis or the Discovery of the Brotherhood of the Honorable Order of the Rosecrucians to the Leaders, Social Classes, and Educated People of Europe," Kassel, 1614. In that text, it reads as follows:

Ex Deo nascimur

In Jesu morimur

Per spiritum reviviscimus.

The changes to the Latin text are from Rudolf Steiner. The literal translation, "We are born out of God, we die in Christ, we are born again through the Holy Spirit" was changed a number of times by Rudolf Steiner. A further translation is found at the end of the lecture given in Vienna on June 11, 1922, in *The Sun Mystery and the Mystery of Death and Resurrection*, CW 211.

Page 232, "The Four Maxims of the Wisdom of the Pillars"
Two columns standing in the hall where the Munich Pentecost Congress of 1907 each bore two verses. The left column was red and the right was blue-red, symbolizing the circulatory system of the human being. Above the verses on the left column stood the letter J for *Jachim,* and above the verses on the right column stood the letter B for *Boaz.* The designation "The Four Maxims of the Wisdom of the Pillars" was originally in Rudolf Steiner's report of the Congress in "Lucifer-Gnosis." For more detailed information see "The Munich Congress" in *Rosicrucianism Renewed,* CW 284, as well as E.S. Berlin, November 1, 1907, in *Esoteric Lessons: 1904-1909,* CW 266/1.

Page 233, "Malsch Foundation Stone Document"
The text in Notebook 532 is in shorthand; the words *geistigt* and *umwebt* in the eighth and eleventh lines are not completely legible. The names of the people who presumably signed the document are found in *Bilder okkulter Siegel und Säulen,* GA 284, p. 180. In English, see *Rosicrucianism Renewed,* CW 284;

Page 235, "Spirit of the Universe"
This verse was discussed in the dedication speech: "When we remember that we wish to be servants of the spirit through the word in this building, which is meant to be an expression of the spirit in its symbols and forms, then a word will resound in our souls. The word is albeit in a somewhat changed form, transferred into our theosophical thoughts; it is a word that has taken hold of and uplifted countless hearts, which have brought together all that they could spare to build a temple dedicated to the spirit, whom they serve. And he who was able to serve, personally, during the building of this temple, spoke these words, which we may translate into our language: 'Spirit of the Universe...' I would have to reach for the words of the Old Testament, for the words of Solomon, in order to express what we ourselves direct, like a prayer, to the spirit of the universe who lives in all hearts

that strive for true self knowledge, arising out of the spirit of human development, which has progressed along with the world." This refers to Solomon's prayer at the dedication of the temple in Jerusalem, 1Kings 8:26. Rudolf Steiner's words are far more than a simple translation, however.

Page 239, "The Foundation Stone document for the building in Dornach, 1913"
Rudolf Steiner transferred this version onto the actual document on the day of the laying of the foundation stone. Count Lerchenfeld had provided the parchment from the skin of a one-year-old steer calf. It was signed by the following people: Carl Schmid, master builder, Leadership Council of the Johannes Building Society; Sophie Stinde, Emil Grosheintz, Herman Linde, Dr. Felix Peipers, Countess Pauline von Kalckreuth, Emmy von Gumppenberg, Lucie Bürgi, Marie Schieb, Marie Hirter-Weber, Executive Board of the Anthroposophical Society; Marie von Sivers, Dr. Carl Unger, Dr. Rudolf Steiner as spiritual leader of the action. The foundation stone consists of two interwoven copper dodecahedra, and contains the document.

Page 241, "The Macrocosmic Lord's Prayer"
As the "macrocosmic counter-image of the microcosmic prayer, the Christian Lord's Prayer, this was first given at the laying of the foundation stone of the Dornach building on September 20, 1913; see page 334. During the lectures held in Christiania (Oslo) in October 1913, *The Fifth Gospel, From the Akashic Record,* CW 148, Rudolf Steiner mentioned that in the words of this prayer are the "original teaching of pagan humanity on the secret of the [literal] incorporation [embodiment] of the human being into earthly-physical corporeality." It is also mentioned that these words represent an extraordinarily meaningful formulation for meditation.

Page 242, "Words on the Window Themes "
This was written for the etchings made by Assja Turgenieff between 1919 and 1922 for the window themes of the Goetheanum. See *Die Goetheanum-Fenster [The Windows of the Goetheanum]*, GA K 12.

Page 247, "Who striving seek to entrust themselves to the light"
The conclusion of the speech at the opening celebration of the first college course at the first Goetheanum, Dornach, September 26, 1920. Manuscript Archive #3997a was retained by Dr. Roman Boos, the initiator and organizer of the college course.

Page 249, "The heavenly beings of the stars /coming close to me"
The chronicle on the plaque burned along with the building. For facsimiles of both drafts in Notebook 212; see GA 219, 6th edition, 1994. In English, *Man and the World of the Stars,* Anthroposophic Press, New York 1982; facsimiles not included. The designation "Spiritual Communion" was added by Marie Steiner.

Page 250, "The power of the waves of the worlds surges"
These two verses stand in Notebook B212 with the verses "The heavenly beings of the stars/coming close to me..." (on the previous page in this volume), for the lecture held on December 31, 1922. A facsimile is found in GA 219.

Page 253, "See the Logos"
In Notebook 570 the last line reads: "In Artemis' house."

Page 254, "The ideal-spiritual laying of the Foundation Stone"
As in the laying of the foundation stone of the Dornach building in 1913, when a double dodecahedron was sunk into the earth (see page 238), so too for the *"ideal-spiritual laying of the foundation stone"* to mark the re-establishment of the Anthroposophical Society at Christmas 1923, a foundation stone in verse form, in a double image, was sunk "into the hearts and souls of the people joined together in the Society." In the lecture on December 25, Rudolf Steiner spoke of the "human dodecahedron" and the "world dodecahedron."

Corresponding to this configuration, Rudolf Steiner spoke the individual verses at the festive laying of the foundation stone of the General Anthroposophical Society, on December 25, 1923, in this way:

First, the three invocations of the human soul as the expression of the human dodecahedron; and subsequently, "to summarize everything," the verse reminding us of the first Christmas, in which the entrance of the light of Christ into the earthly stream of being brought about the turning point in time. Following this, the threefold human dodecahedron verse was repeated and connected with the threefold verse of the world dodecahedron, which addresses the strengths of the heights, the encompassing circle, and the depths.

In the following days, portions of the verses were spoken and explained in various ways. Rudolf Steiner spoke the Foundation Verse in its entirety and in the final order for the first time in his concluding lecture on January 1, 1924, in the evening. Shortly thereafter it was printed in the *Nachrichtenblatt* [*Newsletter*] in that format.

The version given here, as spoken on December 25, follows the pieces of paper numbered by Rudolf Steiner and used on that occasion. The second version was reproduced (from his manuscript) for publication in the *Nachrichtenblatt.* Both versions can be found as facsimiles in the supplement to *Die Weihnachtstagung... [The Christmas Conference]*, GA 260, 5th edition, 1994.

Page 261, "At the turning point of times"
The handwritten text for the first publication in the *Nachrichtenblatt*, Archive #3254, ends with: "Whatever we wish to lead out of our minds." This is placed on the very edge of the paper, and perhaps it was "intended" that this would then be lost. Marie Steiner included this again in her 1935 edition.

A further variation was spoken in the lecture on December 31, 1923: "What we / base upon our hearts / we wish to lead out of our heads, full of light."

Page 263, "In this house"
In the copy in Note A 4529, the signatures are not noted.

Page 264, "May that rule"
According to the transcript of the speech made on December 16, 1921, the foundation stone document was signed by people from the following groups: master builder, architect, faculty, Waldorf school association, supervisory council

and board of directors of the Coming Day, and the Association for the Threefold Social Order. According to Karl Schubert, Rudolf Steiner signed for several who were absent. These are the names:

Emil Molt, Emil Weippert, Rudolf Steiner, Marie Steiner, Karl Stockmeyer, Paul Baumann, Christoph Boy, Martha Haebler, Maria Unland, Berta Molt, Walter Johannes Stein, Ernst Uehli, Elisabeth von Grunelius, Caroline von Heydebrand, Clara Düberg, Helene Rommel, Violetta Plincke, Hedwig Hauck, Edith Röhrle, Julie Lämmert, Robert Killian, Rudolf Treichler, Wilhelm Ruhtenberg, Herbert Hahn, Max Wolffhügel, Karl Schubert, Johannes Geyer, Nora Stein von Baditz, Hermann von Baravalle, Eugen Kolisko, Erich Schwebsch, Maria Röschl, Elisabeth Baumann-Dollfus, Leonie von Mirbach, Rudolf Zoeppritz, Carl Unger, Jose DelMonte, Rudolf Maier, Eugen Benkendörfer, Emil Leinhas, Konradin Hausser, and Hans Kühn. (Marie Steiner officially belonged to the College of Teachers, because she was responsible for eurythmy.)

Page 272, "Out of the light-filled heights of the spirit"
Also given after WW I for the "Seeker Group," led by Miss Pethick.

Page 279, "Human beings see"
Berlin colleague Anna Samweber asked Rudolf Steiner for help in November, 1923, in anticipation of difficult times coming for Berlin.

Page 286, "Where do I find the good?"
For more information, see M.P. van Deventer, "The Anthroposophical-Medical Movement at the Different Stages of Its Development," Arlesheim, 1982.

Page 288, "You healing spirits"
In the notebook, the second line of the second stanza reads: "In the ascent of Mercury." It could also be read as "In the ascending of Mercury." The text on the board has not been preserved, but it was probably copied from the board into the transcript, which reads: "In the ascent of Mercury."

Page 290, "Experience the fire"
This is in the notebook between outlines for the medical course of January, 1924, GA 316. In English, *Understanding Healing,* CW 316, Rudolf Steiner Press, UK 2013.

Page 295, "Feel in the fever's measure / Saturn's spiritual gift"
On the Manuscript Archive page 1272b, the next to last line begins with "And then you will behold..." rather than "And then you will see...."

Page 297, "Feel thinking!"
This is on the same notepaper as the previous verse, "Move the child's early years...."

Page 299, "Mercury-Raphael spoke"
In one of her notebooks (see J.E. Zeylmans van Emmichoven, *Wer war Ita Wegman* Vol. 2, p. 216. In English, *Who Was Ita Wegmen?* Vol. II, Mercury Press, NY.) Ita Wegman describes how she came to Rudolf Steiner in September 1924, shortly before he became ill, with the question: "Couldn't we create a study

of medicine based on the mysteries?" (On p. 216 the question reads: "Is it not possible to found a medical mystery school?") His answer was: It is not so simple. The spiritual world must want it to happen, and people must be present who will accept it. [p. 207:

> After some days he said to me that he had asked the spirit Raphael-Mercury, and received a positive answer, to renew the old practice[s] at a holy and worthy site. This task would be given to him. And to me would be given the task of seeking sensible, spirit-bearing human souls who would be willing to listen to the words of Raphael.
>
> We then began in a very small way, which could not be completed because Rudolf Steiner left the physical plane, and later the necessary maturity and readiness for such a deeply esoteric course of action was not there. When I tell this story, I do not mean that we were able to continue with what once existed. That is not possible, though all of us have a longing for a medical practice based on the mysteries.

In the speech for the physicians in Dornach on September 18, 1924, in GA 318 (In English, see *Broken Vessels, The Spiritual Structure of Human Frailty*, Great Barrington, MA 2003), is the following reference to this "small beginning": "The fact that a first step was taken was reason enough for Dr. Wegman and me to give a first esoteric impulse to that, so that an esoteric core has been formed—one that can absolutely be expanded upon. For the present, it consists only of a certain number of practical physicians who have achieved the necessary initiation, which is essential for the effectiveness of an esoteric medical practice. This central core consists of the following practical physicians: Dr. Walter, Dr. Bockholt, Dr. Zeylmans, Dr. Glas, Dr. Schickler, Dr. Knauer, and Dr. Kolisko..."

Page 300, "May there dwell in hearts"
See also the essay by Ita Wegman: "The Nursing School in Dornach" [*Die Schwesternschule in Dornach*]" in the *Newsletter* [*Nachrichtenblatt*], May 10, 1925: "Thereafter, Rudolf Steiner proposed that the nurses form an association. His intention of opening the nursing school himself with a lecture course could not be carried out."

Page 301, "To live in the spirit"
The passage from the letter to Paul Klein that belongs to this verse reads as follows: "In your spiritual life situation (I say this to you as a friend), you must set the relationship of your own self to the spiritual world as the primary and highest content of your life. By this I do not mean only a visionary relationship, but also a mystic-religious relationship, mediated through the living Christ. This relationship must be felt so securely that it is like the Sun of life, which has, with respect to everything else, and it is well-justified—still has a planetary existence. "To live in the spirit..." "He for whom it is predetermined, that he shall prepare a place on Earth for the spirit, will find himself experiencing this sentiment and attitude...."

Page 303, "With a feeling of need"
Given the similarity in the content and form of the loose note sheet with the

meditation "To you, carrier of the word of the worlds..." written for Pastor Paul Klein, it is quite probable that this verse was a preliminary version for the meditation.

Page 306, "The awareness fills me"
In the draft Archive #3589a, lines 7-8 read:

"I see the spirit of the Sun and the soul of the Moon
I speak the word of God to the ears of Earth."

Page 312, "In what had come over from Saturn, Sun, and Moon existences"
Marie Steiner lightly edited this passage from the transcript of the lecture for recitation.

Page 320, "In the primal beginning was the Word"
The text reprinted here, verses 1-18, appeared in its entirety for the first time in *Das Johannes-Evangelium* (GA 103), lecture of May 22, 1908, Hamburg. In English, see *The Gospel of St. John,* Anthroposophic Press, Hudson, NY 1984.

Earlier, in 1906, verses 1-14 appeared with the same wording (including the parenthetical additions) in lecture of October 27, 1906, Munich, in *Kosmogonie* (GA 94). In English, see *An Esoteric Cosmology,* SteinerBooks, Great Barrington MA 2008.

Still earlier, in 1904, verses 1-14 appeared for the first time (without the parenthetical additions) in the lecture given in Berlin on July 11, 1904, for which the handwritten notes (Archive #3477-78) are extant. This lecture has not yet been published.

Page 324, "In the beginning is memory"
In the first edition of the lecture of March 7, 1914, Pforzheim, (Dornach 1930), the first line (following the transcript available at the time) reads as follows: "In the beginning he lives..." (and it also appears in this form in the 1935 edition of *Warspruchworte* [*Verses and Meditations,* Rudolf Steiner Press, Bristol UK 1993]. This is based on a transcribing error of the stenographer, who read an abbreviation incorrectly. Other transcriptions, which reached the Archive later, show this line correctly.

Page 331, "The Esoteric (Apostles') Lord's Prayer"
According to Marie Steiner, Rudolf Steiner referred to this prayer as "the esoteric Lord's Prayer or the Lord's Prayer of the Apostles" (in a letter answering a question on this topic, written on July 4, 1938). A manuscript from her bears the title "The Esoteric (Apostles') Lord's Prayer." It was apparently given only to a very small circle of people. Some of the handwritten texts available in the Rudolf Steiner Archive, written by members of the Esoteric School from 1904 to 1914, point out that the "very small circle of people" must have been connected with the Esoteric School.

No original, handwritten manuscript from Rudolf Steiner is available. Possibly there never was one, since all surviving texts, even those in Marie Steiner's handwriting, show minor variations. A plea, or request, is missing in all of these versions. Cornelius E. de Jong, of Holland, reported this on January 14, 1965, in a letter to Edwin Froböse, who was attempting to clear up questions about the origin of the text at the time: On February 20, 1913, he visited Mrs. Paula van Deventer in Arnheim. At the same time, Miss A. Roelofs appeared, having come from Berlin, and reported that Rudolf Steiner and Miss von Sivers (Marie Steiner) would stay in the Knottenbelt's house in The Hague while events were being held there, from March 18-29. The precise wording of the letter was as follows: "Miss A. Roelofs then gave a piece of paper to Mrs. van Deventer, who gave it to me after reading it. I read it through carefully, and then returned it to Miss A. Roelofs, remarking: 'There is a line missing!' After that, doubt and consternation turned into agreement. The fact could not be denied. When the question came, asking what we should do, I suggested that we ask Miss Alex Knottenbelt to ask Dr. Steiner personally (who would soon be staying in the Knottenbelt's home for a period of time) about the missing line. And that was done. Not until nearly the end of that time in The Hague did I receive the (apparently) missing line from Mrs. P. van Deventer. When I asked her for more specific information about how that had happened, this is what I found out: One afternoon, as Dr. Steiner entered the room with Miss von Sivers, dressed to leave the house, Miss Alex Knottenbelt stepped up to Dr. Steiner, gave him the piece of paper, and asked him about the missing line. Without further ado, he added the sixth line, while Miss von Sivers waited next to him. That is how the whole thing took place. It remains clear in my memory, as do many things which are important to me." The piece of paper with the line added could not, however, be found.

Rudolf Steiner himself appears to have said nothing further about the missing line. For one thing, the Esoteric School was already closed by the middle of 1914. In addition, Rudolf Steiner was present at two burial services held by the Christ-Catholic priest Hugo Schuster for women who were anthroposophists. The women, like Schuster himself, had belonged to the Esoteric School. Schuster added this esoteric Lord's Prayer to the services, along with the usual Lord's Prayer. According to the stenographic transcript made during the services, the wording of the prayer followed the original form, which was also the wording used in the Esoteric School. In this version, the line, "You should not allow the tempter..." with "*Mara*, do not allow the tempter...". Schuster substituted "Satan, the tempter..." for the Indian expression "*Mara*." It is not known whether Rudolf Steiner knew that this was done, or not.

The source for the wording of the sixth line, of the fifth request, thus appears to be de Jong exclusively, who remarked (in the letter from which we quoted): "When people showed me the text at various times and in all sorts of places, then I added the sixth line!"

According to a note from Edwin Froböse, an actor and member of the speaking chorus of the Goetheanum stage, trained by Marie Steiner, the chorus worked on this version of the Lord's Prayer in the years following Rudolf Steiner's death: "It was spoken on very special occasions." For this purpose, Marie Steiner had apparently copied the text on a particular sheet of paper (Handwritten note A 5367), from which it is apparent that she must have been aware of the missing fifth request, but did not have access to its wording. Thus the prayer was spoken by the chorus without this request, which explains why Edwin Froböse did not know it.

On the wording: because there is no original manuscript from Rudolf Steiner, the wording used here is that found in most of the sources. Variations: some handwritten sources (presumably those written the earliest, chronologically speaking, from Marie Steiner and other members of the Esoteric School) have "*Aum* Amen" at the beginning and the end. In addition, the line "the tempter..." begins with "*Mara*, the tempter..." and rather than "the tempter is only..." it reads "*Mara* is only...". Further very minor variations can be ascribed solely to changes made as copies were made over the years: Line 2: "praised [*lobgepriesen*]"; Line 3: "in the course of our lives [*in unseren Lebensläufen*]"; Line 4: "into our innermost being [*in unser innerstes Wesen*]"; Line 5: "you give us [*gibst du uns*]"; Line 6: "Let there be a balance in our compassion for people for the guilt, into which we in our existence have fallen [*Lasse Ausgleich sein unser Erbarmen an Menschen für die Schuld, der wir in unserem Wesen verfallen*]" (questionable, since no other source other than de Jong is known); Line 7: only in Schuster's version: "Satan, the tempter,... for Satan is only illusory [*Satan, den Versucher...denn Satan ist nur Schein...*]"

Page 332, "The Lord's Prayer in the Wulfila Bible"

The Gothic Lord's Prayer: This Lord's Prayer stems from the Bible translation made by the Gothic [Eastern Germanic] bishop Wulfila (Ulfilas, 310-383 C.E.) and was read by Rudolf Steiner in the Dornach lecture on May 15, 1921, in GA 325, *Die Naturwissenschaft und die weltgeschichtliche Entwicklung der Menschheit seit dem Altertum [Natural Science and the World-Historical Development of Humankind Since Antiquity].* In Rudolf Steiner's Notebook 96 concerning these lectures, only the Gothic text is to be found. The German translation came into being during the lecture. The portion of the lecture concerned with the Lord's Prayer was as follows:

And we notice and sense this early spiritual development most intensively, when we take the book into our hands, which is left to us as an ancient Gothic memorial: Wulfila's translation of the Bible. And if we have a sense for this, for allowing the spirit of this Bible translation to work on our souls, it appears remarkable how the Lord's Prayer, for example, is constructed out of residual vestiges [of decaying ancient culture], out of all of the confusion for which Augustine set the tone. And the Lord's Prayer out of Wulfila's Bible translation resounds in us, though it emerged out of an entirely elementary, ancient social life—from Arian Christianity, in contrast to the Athanasian Christianity of Augustine.

Yes, from the style of Wulfila's Bible translation, more so than from anything else from the time, we can sense the heathen (if I may call it that) spirit alive at that time, which was being intensively intermingled with Christianity at the time—Arian Christianity, to be sure. If we take note of all aspects of the situation, we can sense which spirit lived in this simple Gothic bishop, Wulfila, who translated the Bible. One need only observe the situation with sensitivity. These barbaric masses, moving westward out of the East, provided something to fill in the gap left by the downfall of ancient Roman education and culture.

We sense that something wonderful was alive in their spiritual life, their Gothic spiritual life, which lived in their teacher, as well; lived in Wulfila's manner of praying the Lord's Prayer:

Atta unsar thu in himinam,
weihnai namo thein.
Qimai thiudinassus theins.
Wairthai wilja theins, swe in himina jah ana aerthai.
Hlaif unsarana thana sinteinan gif uns himma daga.
Jah aflet uns thatei skulans sijaima, swaswe jah weis afletam thaim skulam unsaraim. Jah ni briggais uns in fraistubnjai, ak lausei uns af thamma ubilin; unte theina ist thiudangardi jah mahts jah wulthus in aiwins. Amen.

Atta unsar thu in himinam, weihnai namo thein; Qimai thiudinassus theins. Wairthai Wilja theins, swe in himina, jah ana aerthai. Now when we look through this wonderful prayer in the language of Wulfila, and attempt to translate it into the language of today, we cannot translate literally, but must say something like this:

We sense you above there in the spiritual heights,
All-Father of humankind.
Hallowed be your name.
May the realm of your dominion come to us.
May your will rule on the Earth, as it does in heaven.

And we must have a proper sense for what is being expressed. The human being who translated the Lord's Prayer in this way experienced something truly ancient, which was essentially what all ancient heathens experienced: the all-sustaining Father of humanity in the spiritual heights, whom one imagined in a way that the older clairvoyance permitted—as a king; an invisible, suprasensory king who rules over his dominion as no earthly king might. Among the free Goths, he was addressed as a king, and that was expressed in the line: *Atta unsar thu in himinam.* And then they addressed his threefold being: "Hallowed be your name." With the name itself, it was understood that one referred to the being and his existence; one need only compare this with the meaning of ancient Sanskrit expressions. And not only the being, but how the being expresses itself, how it manifests itself toward others, similar to the way the human being manifests himself in his bodily being. The words "realm of your dominion" were understood to be what lay within his power, even within his might and control, which could exercise command and control in the [earthly] territory, as well: *weihnai namo thein. Qimai thiudinassus theins. Wairthai wilja theins, swe in himina jah ana aerthai.*

By using the term "will," they understood the power and name shining through the spirit. They directed their gaze upward and saw the threefold spirituality ruling supreme in the spirit of the suprasensory worlds. They raised themselves up before this spirit, and then said: *jah ana aerthai. Hlaif unsarana thana sinteinan gif uns himma daga.* Just as it is on Earth. How is it on Earth? Just as your name, which you use to manifest yourself, should be holy, as you are, so may that aspect of us, which manifests itself to the outer world, and must be renewed daily, may that also be illuminated. One must understand what meaning lies in the ancient Gothic word *hlaif*, the word that became our word for loaf; loaf of bread. We no longer have a feeling for the way things were, when we now say "Give us today our daily bread," since here, the word *hlaif* means "As we allow your name to mean 'the body,' let our bodies take on this aspect, so that they can be nourished each day through the food we take in through our metabolism."

And the prayer then transitions to "the realm of dominion" from which God should rule, from suprasensory worlds, and it transitions in precisely the same way to what reigns among human beings in the social order. In that heavenly realm, as the Goths understood it, no one is the debtor of another. The word "debt" bore a particular meaning among the Goths, a concrete meaning of being indebted to someone in the social realm, in the moral as well as the physical sense.

The transition was made, then, as one moved from the name to the heavenly realm, so too from the body to the spirit. In the suprasensory realm, the name signifies nearly the same thing as the physical body. Thus as one transitioned from the soul realm to the heavenly realm, one moved from the external-physical to what is spiritual within social life, and then moved to the truly spiritual: "Let us not degenerate." *Jah aflet uns, thatei skulans sijaima, swaswe jah weis afletam thaim skulam unsaraim.* Which means: "So that we do not become the debtors of one another in our social lives, so that we stand across from one another as equal human beings, so that we do not decline with the bodily-spiritual." *Jah ni briggais uns in fraistubnjai, ak lausei uns af thamma ubilin.* "Let us not degenerate into the aspect of our being which brings our spirit into darkness, but deliver us from the evils, which arise when we threaten to lapse too strongly into our physical selves with our spirit."

So, for all practical purposes, the second section expresses the idea that there should be an order to social life on Earth which corresponds to that up in heaven, in the spiritual heights. And this is reinforced yet again: we want to recognize this sort of spiritual order here on Earth. *Unte theina ist thiudangardi, jah mahts, jah wulthus in aiwins.* Amen.

Father of all, whose name forms the external corporeality of the spirit, whose realm of dominion we wish to honor and recognize, whose will should rule, you, you should also permeate the earthly realm, so that we see our bodily selves again each day, see them arise again anew each day, to some degree, through the nourishment available on Earth. We do not wish to be indebted to others in the social realm, but to stand across from one another as equals. We do not wish to lapse too far into the spiritual-corporeal. We wish to link the trinity of the earthly social realm with the suprasensory; for the suprasensory should rule, should be king and emperor. Not something from the sensory world, not something personal on Earth, but rather the suprasensory should rule.

Unte theina ist thiudangardi, jah mahts, jah vulthus in aiwins. Amen. The right to rule belongs not to a thing, and not to a being here on Earth, but to you; yours is the right to power, yours is the manifestation as light, as a glow, as social love which reigns over all. This trinity of the suprasensory is expressed in a threefold way, how it should permeate into the sensory social order. And once again, at the end, this is strengthened, because these words are added: Yes, we wish to have this in our social structure, that the trinity should be felt on Earth just as it is in the heavens, with you, for yours is the right to rule, yours is the right to power, yours is the revelation: *Theina ist thiudangardi, jah mahts, jah vulthus in aiwins*. Amen.

This is what resounded and echoed in the minds of these Goths; this is what ruled in the background, what now came forward like a force of nature after the downfall of the ancient culture. And out of what arose as something natural, and was then pushed down again; what mixed itself with the rusticity of the times and the simple people whose perceptions were barely recorded by history; what evolved after ancient culture smoldered and found itself extinguished in the fourth century after Christ now moved forward to what became lost to view in the eyes of history until the beginning of the fifteenth century, which kindled something that developed slowly at first, then ever more rapidly in the nineteenth century, that it led to a huge spiritual change in direction, which we have characterized today [in the lecture].

Page 334, "Address at the Laying of the Foundation Stone of the Dornach Building "

This speech, held in connection with the celebration at the laying of the foundation stone, written very much in the style of an esoteric lesson, was published by Marie Steiner in *Aus den Inhalten der Esoterischen Schule [From the Contents of the Esoteric School]*. The text of the speech (albeit with gaps) remains available to us only by pure luck and happenstance, because Rudolf Hahn, the member who knew shorthand and participated, attempted to write as much as possible using the back of the person standing next to him. Conditions were not favorable for writing: the weather was poor and the lighting was provided by torches, for the ceremony took place at the end of September from 6:30 p.m. to approximately 8:30 p.m. in the excavated area.

Page 338, "As the first aspect of the Fifth Gospel"

On the second day following the laying of the foundation stone, Rudolf Steiner traveled to Oslo to hold the planned cycle of lectures *The Fifth Gospel—From the Akashic Record* (CW 148). In the lectures on October 5 and 6, he spoke extensively about the macrocosmic Lord's Prayer.

Page 339, "as human beings who manifest the light of the spirit through the power of thought, even when the sinister Ahriman wishes to spread the darkness of chaos"

These are the final words of the fourth drama, "The Awakening of Souls," in *Four Mystery Dramas*, CW 14.

RUDOLF STEINER'S COLLECTED WORKS

The German Edition of Rudolf Steiner's Collected Works (the *Gesamtausgabe* [GA] published by Rudolf Steiner Verlag, Dornach, Switzerland) presently runs to 354 titles, organized either by type of work (written or spoken), chronology, audience (public or other), or subject (education, art, etc.). For ease of comparison, the Collected Works in English [CW] follows the German organization. A complete listing of the CWs follows with *literal translations* of the German titles. Other than in the case of the books published in his lifetime, titles were rarely given by Rudolf Steiner himself, and were often provided by the editors of the German editions. The titles in English are not necessarily the same as the German; and, indeed, over the past seventy-five years have frequently been different, with the same book sometimes appearing under different titles.

For ease of identification and to avoid confusion, we suggest that readers looking for a title should do so by CW number. Because the work of creating the Collected Works of Rudolf Steiner is an ongoing process, with new titles being published every year, we have not indicated in this listing which books are presently available. To find out what titles in the Collected Works are currently in print, please check our website at www.steinerbooks.org, or write to: SteinerBooks; 610 Main Street, Great Barrington, MA 01230.

A. Written Works

I. Writings 1884–1925

CW 1 Goethe: Natural-Scientific Writings, Introduction, with Footnotes and Explanations in the text by Rudolf Steiner

CW 2 Outlines of an Epistemology of the Goethean World View, with Special Consideration of Schiller

CW 3 Truth and Science

CW 4 The Philosophy of Freedom

CW 4a Documents to "The Philosophy of Freedom"

CW 5 Friedrich Nietzsche, A Fighter against His Own Time

CW 6 Goethe's Worldview

CW 6a *[Now in CW 30]*

CW 7 Mysticism at the Dawn of Modern Spiritual Life and Its Relationship with Modern Worldviews

CW 8 Christianity as Mystical Fact and the Mysteries of Antiquity

CW 9 Theosophy: An Introduction into Supersensible World Knowledge and Human Purpose

CW 10 How Does One Attain Knowledge of Higher Worlds?

CW 11 From the Akasha-Chronicle

CW 12 Levels of Higher Knowledge

CW 13 Occult Science in Outline

CW 14 Four Mystery Dramas

CW 15	The Spiritual Guidance of the Individual and Humanity
CW 16	A Way to Human Self-Knowledge: Eight Meditations
CW 17	The Threshold of the Spiritual World. Aphoristic Comments
CW 18	The Riddles of Philosophy in Their History, Presented as an Outline
CW 19	*[Contained in CW 24]*
CW 20	The Riddles of the Human Being: Articulated and Unarticulated in the Thinking, Views and Opinions of a Series of German and Austrian Personalities
CW 21	The Riddles of the Soul
CW 22	Goethe's Spiritual Nature and Its Revelation in "Faust" and through the "Fairy Tale of the Snake and the Lily"
CW 23	The Central Points of the Social Question in the Necessities of Life in the Present and the Future
CW 24	Essays Concerning the Threefold Division of the Social Organism and the Period 1915-1921
CW 25	Cosmology, Religion and Philosophy
CW 26	Anthroposophical Leading Thoughts
CW 27	Fundamentals for Expansion of the Art of Healing according to Spiritual-Scientific Insights
CW 28	The Course of My Life

II. Collected Essays

CW 29	Collected Essays on Dramaturgy, 1889-1900
CW 30	Methodical Foundations of Anthroposophy: Collected Essays on Philosophy, Natural Science, Aesthetics and Psychology, 1884-1901
CW 31	Collected Essays on Culture and Current Events, 1887-1901
CW 32	Collected Essays on Literature, 1884-1902
CW 33	Biographies and Biographical Sketches, 1894-1905
CW 34	Lucifer-Gnosis: Foundational Essays on Anthroposophy and Reports from the Periodicals "Lucifer" and "Lucifer-Gnosis," 1903-1908
CW 35	Philosophy and Anthroposophy: Collected Essays, 1904-1923
CW 36	The Goetheanum-Idea in the Middle of the Cultural Crisis of the Present: Collected Essays from the Periodical "Das Goetheanum," 1921-1925
CW 37	*[Now in CWs 251 and 260a]*

III. Publications from the Literary Estate

CW 38	Letters, Vol. 1: 1881-1890
CW 39	Letters, Vol. 2: 1890-1925
CW 40	Truth-Wrought Words
CW 40a	Sayings, Poems and Mantras; Supplementary Volume
CW 42	*[Now in CWs 264-266]*

CW 43 Stage Adaptations
CW 44 On the Four Mystery Dramas. Sketches, Fragments and Paralipomena on the Four Mystery Dramas
CW 45 Anthroposophy: A Fragment from the Year 1910

B. Lectures

I. Public Lectures

CW 51 On Philosophy, History and Literature
CW 52 Spiritual Teachings Concerning the Soul and Observation of the World
CW 53 The Origin and Goal of the Human Being
CW 54 The Riddles of the World and Anthroposophy
CW 55 Knowledge of the Supersensible in Our Times and Its Meaning for Life Today
CW 56 Knowledge of the Soul and of the Spirit
CW 57 Where and How Does One Find the Spirit?
CW 58 The Metamorphoses of the Soul Life. Paths of Soul Experiences: Part One
CW 59 The Metamorphoses of the Soul Life. Paths of Soul Experiences: Part Two
CW 60 The Answers of Spiritual Science to the Biggest Questions of Existence
CW 61 Human History in the Light of Spiritual Research
CW 62 Results of Spiritual Research
CW 63 Spiritual Science as a Treasure for Life
CW 64 Out of Destiny-Burdened Times
CW 65 Out of Central European Spiritual Life
CW 66 Spirit and Matter, Life and Death
CW 67 The Eternal in the Human Soul. Immortality and Freedom
CW 68 Public lectures in various cities, 1906-1918
CW 69 Public lectures in various cities, 1906-1918
CW 70 Public lectures in various cities, 1906-1918
CW 71 Public lectures in various cities, 1906-1918
CW 72 Freedom – Immortality – Social Life
CW 73 The Supplementing of the Modern Sciences through Anthroposophy
CW 73a Specialized Fields of Knowledge and Anthroposophy
CW 74 The Philosophy of Thomas Aquinas
CW 75 Public lectures in various cities, 1906-1918
CW 76 The Fructifying Effect of Anthroposophy on Specialized Fields
CW 77a The Task of Anthroposophy in Relation to Science and Life: The Darmstadt College Course

CW 77b Art and Anthroposophy. The Goetheanum-Impulse
CW 78 Anthroposophy, Its Roots of Knowledge and Fruits for Life
CW 79 The Reality of the Higher Worlds
CW 80 Public lectures in various cities, 1922
CW 81 Renewal-Impulses for Culture and Science–Berlin College Course
CW 82 So that the Human Being Can Become a Complete Human Being
CW 83 Western and Eastern World-Contrast. Paths to Understanding It through Anthroposophy
CW 84 What Did the Goetheanum Intend and What Should Anthroposophy Do?

II. Lectures to the Members of the Anthroposophical Society

CW 88 Concerning the Astral World and Devachan
CW 89 Consciousness – Life – Form. Fundamental Principles of a Spiritual-Scientific Cosmology
CW 90 Participant Notes from the Lectures during the Years 1903-1905
CW 91 Participant Notes from the Lectures during the Years 1903-1905
CW 92 The Occult Truths of Ancient Myths and Sagas
CW 93 The Temple Legend and the Golden Legend
CW 93a Fundamentals of Esotericism
CW 94 Cosmogony. Popular Occultism. The Gospel of John. The Theosophy in the Gospel of John
CW 95 At the Gates of Theosophy
CW 96 Origin-Impulses of Spiritual Science. Christian Esotericism in the Light of New Spirit-Knowledge
CW 97 The Christian Mystery
CW 98 Nature Beings and Spirit Beings – Their Effects in Our Visible World
CW 99 The Theosophy of the Rosicrucians
CW 100 Human Development and Christ-Knowledge
CW 101 Myths and Legends. Occult Signs and Symbols
CW 102 The Working into Human Beings by Spiritual Beings
CW 103 The Gospel of John
CW 104 The Apocalypse of John
CW 104a From the Picture-Script of the Apocalypse of John
CW 105 Universe, Earth, the Human Being: Their Being and Development, as well as Their Reflection in the Connection between Egyptian Mythology and Modern Culture
CW 106 Egyptian Myths and Mysteries in Relation to the Active Spiritual Forces of the Present
CW 107 Spiritual-Scientific Knowledge of the Human Being
CW 108 Answering the Questions of Life and the World through Anthroposophy

CW 109 The Principle of Spiritual Economy in Connection with the Question of Reincarnation. An Aspect of the Spiritual Guidance of Humanity
CW 110 The Spiritual Hierarchies and Their Reflection in the Physical World. Zodiac, Planets and Cosmos
CW 111 *[Contained in CW 109]*
CW 112 The Gospel of John in Relation to the Three Other Gospels, Especially the Gospel of Luke
CW 113 The Orient in the Light of the Occident. The Children of Lucifer and the Brothers of Christ
CW 114 The Gospel of Luke
CW 115 Anthroposophy – Psychosophy – Pneumatosophy
CW 116 The Christ-Impulse and the Development of "I"- Consciousness
CW 117 The Deeper Secrets of the Development of Humanity in Light of the Gospels
CW 118 The Event of the Christ-Appearance in the Etheric World
CW 119 Macrocosm and Microcosm. The Large World and the Small World. Soul-Questions, Life-Questions, Spirit-Questions
CW 120 The Revelation of Karma
CW 121 The Mission of Individual Folk-Souls in Connection with Germanic-Nordic Mythology
CW 122 The Secrets of the Biblical Creation-Story. The Six-Day Work in the First Book of Moses
CW 123 The Gospel of Matthew
CW 124 Excursus in the Area of the Gospel of Mark
CW 125 Paths and Goals of the Spiritual Human Being. Life Questions in the Light of Spiritual Science
CW 126 Occult History. Esoteric Observations of the Karmic Relationships of Personalities and Events of World History
CW 127 The Mission of the New Spiritual Revelation. The Christ-Event as the Middle-Point of Earth Evolution
CW 128 An Occult Physiology
CW 129 Wonders of the World, Trials of the Soul, and Revelations of the Spirit
CW 130 Esoteric Christianity and the Spiritual Guidance of Humanity
CW 131 From Jesus to Christ
CW 132 Evolution from the View Point of the Truth
CW 133 The Earthly and the Cosmic Human Being
CW 134 The World of the Senses and the World of the Spirit
CW 135 Reincarnation and Karma and their Meaning for the Culture of the Present
CW 136 The Spiritual Beings in Celestial Bodies and the Realms of Nature
CW 137 The Human Being in the Light of Occultism, Theosophy and Philosophy

CW 138	On Initiation. On Eternity and the Passing Moment. On the Light of the Spirit and the Darkness of Life
CW 139	The Gospel of Mark
CW 140	Occult Investigation into the Life between Death and New Birth. The Living Interaction between Life and Death
CW 141	Life between Death and New Birth in Relationship to Cosmic Facts
CW 142	The Bhagavad Gita and the Letters of Paul
CW 143	Experiences of the Supersensible. Three Paths of the Soul to Christ
CW 144	The Mysteries of the East and of Christianity
CW 145	What Significance Does Occult Development of the Human Being Have for the Sheaths – Physical Body, Etheric Body, Astral Body, and Self?
CW 146	The Occult Foundations of the Bhagavad Gita
CW 147	The Secrets of the Threshold
CW 148	Out of Research in the Akasha: The Fifth Gospel
CW 149	Christ and the Spiritual World. Concerning the Search for the Holy Grail
CW 150	The World of the Spirit and Its Extension into Physical Existence; The Influence of the Dead in the World of the Living
CW 151	Human Thought and Cosmic Thought
CW 152	Preliminary Stages to the Mystery of Golgotha
CW 153	The Inner Being of the Human Being and Life Between Death and New Birth
CW 154	How does One Gain an Understanding of the Spiritual World? The Flowing in of Spiritual Impulses from out of the World of the Deceased
CW 155	Christ and the Human Soul. Concerning the Meaning of Life. Theosophical Morality. Anthroposophy and Christianity
CW 156	Occult Reading and Occult Hearing
CW 157	Human Destinies and the Destiny of Peoples
CW 157a	The Formation of Destiny and the Life after Death
CW 158	The Connection Between the Human Being and the Elemental World. Kalevala – Olaf Asteson – The Russian People – The World as the Result of the Influences of Equilibrium
CW 159	The Mystery of Death. The Nature and Significance of Middle Europe and the European Folk Spirits
CW 160	*[In CW 159]*
CW 161	Paths of Spiritual Knowledge and the Renewal of the Artistic Worldview
CW 162	Questions of Art and Life in Light of Spiritual Science
CW 163	Coincidence, Necessity and Providence. Imaginative Knowledge and the Processes after Death

CW 164 The Value of Thinking for a Knowledge That Satisfies the Human Being. The Relationship of Spiritual Science to Natural Science
CW 165 The Spiritual Unification of Humanity through the Christ-Impulse
CW 166 Necessity and Freedom in World Events and in Human Action
CW 167 The Present and the Past in the Human Spirit
CW 168 The Connection between the Living and the Dead
CW 169 World-being and Selfhood
CW 170 The Riddle of the Human Being. The Spiritual Background of Human History. Cosmic and Human History, Vol. 1
CW 171 Inner Development-Impulses of Humanity. Goethe and the Crisis of the 19th Century. Cosmic and Human History, Vol. 2
CW 172 The Karma of the Vocation of the Human Being in Connection with Goethe's Life. Cosmic and Human History, Vol. 3
CW 173 Contemporary-Historical Considerations: The Karma of Untruthfulness, Part One. Cosmic and Human History, Vol. 4
CW 174 Contemporary-Historical Considerations: The Karma of Untruthfulness, Part Two. Cosmic and Human History, Vol. 5
CW 174a Middle Europe between East and West. Cosmic and Human History, Vol. 6
CW 174b The Spiritual Background of the First World War. Cosmic and Human History, Vol. 7
CW 175 Building Stones for an Understanding of the Mystery of Golgotha. Cosmic and Human Metamorphoses
CW 176 Truths of Evolution of the Individual and Humanity. The Karma of Materialism
CW 177 The Spiritual Background of the Outer World. The Fall of the Spirits of Darkness. Spiritual Beings and Their Effects, Vol. 1
CW 178 Individual Spiritual Beings and their Influence in the Soul of the Human Being. Spiritual Beings and their Effects, Vol. 2
CW 179 Spiritual Beings and Their Effects. Historical Necessity and Freedom. The Influences on Destiny from out of the World of the Dead. Spiritual Beings and Their Effects, Vol. 3
CW 180 Mystery Truths and Christmas Impulses. Ancient Myths and their Meaning. Spiritual Beings and Their Effects, Vol. 4
CW 181 Earthly Death and Cosmic Life. Anthroposophical Gifts for Life. Necessities of Consciousness for the Present and the Future.
CW 182 Death as Transformation of Life
CW 183 The Science of the Development of the Human Being
CW 184 The Polarity of Duration and Development in Human Life. The Cosmic Pre-History of Humanity
CW 185 Historical Symptomology
CW 185a Historical-Developmental Foundations for Forming a Social Judgment

CW 186	The Fundamental Social Demands of Our Time–In Changed Situations
CW 187	How Can Humanity Find the Christ Again? The Threefold Shadow-Existence of our Time and the New Christ-Light
CW 188	Goetheanism, a Transformation-Impulse and Resurrection-Thought. Science of the Human Being and Science of Sociology
CW 189	The Social Question as a Question of Consciousness. The Spiritual Background of the Social Question, Vol. 1
CW 190	Impulses of the Past and the Future in Social Occurrences. The Spiritual Background of the Social Question, Vol. 2
CW 191	Social Understanding from Spiritual-Scientific Cognition. The Spiritual Background of the Social Question, Vol. 3
CW 192	Spiritual-Scientific Treatment of Social and Pedagogical Questions
CW 193	The Inner Aspect of the Social Riddle. Luciferic Past and Ahrimanic Future
CW 194	The Mission of Michael. The Revelation of the Actual Mysteries of the Human Being
CW 195	Cosmic New Year and the New Year Idea
CW 196	Spiritual and Social Transformations in the Development of Humanity
CW 197	Polarities in the Development of Humanity: West and East Materialism and Mysticism Knowledge and Belief
CW 198	Healing Factors for the Social Organism
CW 199	Spiritual Science as Knowledge of the Foundational Impulses of Social Formation
CW 200	The New Spirituality and the Christ-Experience of the 20th Century
CW 201	The Correspondences Between Microcosm and Macrocosm. The Human Being – A Hieroglyph of the Universe. The Human Being in Relationship with the Cosmos: 1
CW 202	The Bridge between the World-Spirituality and the Physical Aspect of the Human Being. The Search for the New Isis, the Divine Sophia. The Human Being in Relationship with the Cosmos: 2
CW 203	The Responsibility of Human Beings for the Development of the World through their Spiritual Connection with the Planet Earth and the World of the Stars. The Human Being in Relationship with the Cosmos: 3
CW 204	Perspectives of the Development of Humanity. The Materialistic Knowledge-Impulse and the Task of Anthroposophy. The Human Being in Relationship with the Cosmos: 4
CW 205	Human Development, World-Soul, and World-Spirit. Part One: The Human Being as a Being of Body and Soul in Relationship to the World. The Human Being in Relationship with the Cosmos: 5

CW 206 Human Development, World-Soul, and World-Spirit. Part Two: The Human Being as a Spiritual Being in the Process of Historical Development. The Human Being in Relationship with the Cosmos: 6
CW 207 Anthroposophy as Cosmosophy. Part One: Characteristic Features of the Human Being in the Earthly and the Cosmic Realms. The Human Being in Relationship with the Cosmos: 7
CW 208 Anthroposophy as Cosmosophy. Part Two: The Forming of the Human Being as the Result of Cosmic Influence. The Human Being in Relationship with the Cosmos: 8
CW 209 Nordic and Central European Spiritual Impulses. The Festival of the Appearance of Christ. The Human Being in Relationship with the Cosmos: 9
CW 210 Old and New Methods of Initiation. Drama and Poetry in the Change of Consciousness in the Modern Age
CW 211 The Sun Mystery and the Mystery of Death and Resurrection. Exoteric and Esoteric Christianity
CW 212 Human Soul Life and Spiritual Striving in Connection with World and Earth Development
CW 213 Human Questions and World Answers
CW 214 The Mystery of the Trinity: The Human Being in Relationship with the Spiritual World in the Course of Time
CW 215 Philosophy, Cosmology, and Religion in Anthroposophy
CW 216 The Fundamental Impulses of the World-Historical Development of Humanity
CW 217 Spiritually Active Forces in the Coexistence of the Older and Younger Generations. Pedagogical Course for Youth
CW 217a Youth's Cognitive Task
CW 218 Spiritual Connections in the Forming of the Human Organism
CW 219 The Relationship of the World of the Stars to the Human Being, and of the Human Being to the World of the Stars. The Spiritual Communion of Humanity
CW 220 Living Knowledge of Nature. Intellectual Fall and Spiritual Redemption
CW 221 Earth-Knowing and Heaven-Insight
CW 222 The Imparting of Impulses to World-Historical Events through Spiritual Powers
CW 223 The Cycle of the Year as Breathing Process of the Earth and the Four Great Festival-Seasons. Anthroposophy and the Human Heart (*Gemüt*)
CW 224 The Human Soul and its Connection with Divine-Spiritual Individualities. The Internalization of the Festivals of the Year
CW 225 Three Perspectives of Anthroposophy. Cultural Phenomena observed from a Spiritual-Scientific Perspective
CW 226 Human Being, Human Destiny, and World Development

CW 227	Initiation-Knowledge
CW 228	Science of Initiation and Knowledge of the Stars. The Human Being in the Past, the Present, and the Future from the Viewpoint of the Development of Consciousness
CW 229	The Experiencing of the Course of the Year in Four Cosmic Imaginations
CW 230	The Human Being as Harmony of the Creative, Building, and Formative World-Word
CW 231	The Supersensible Human Being, Understood Anthroposophically
CW 232	The Forming of the Mysteries
CW 233	World History Illuminated by Anthroposophy and as the Foundation for Knowledge of the Human Spirit
CW 233a	Mystery Sites of the Middle Ages: Rosicrucianism and the Modern Initiation-Principle. The Festival of Easter as Part of the History of the Mysteries of Humanity
CW 234	Anthroposophy. A Summary after 21 Years
CW 235	Esoteric Observations of Karmic Relationships in 6 Volumes, Vol. 1
CW 236	Esoteric Observations of Karmic Relationships in 6 Volumes, Vol. 2
CW 237	Esoteric Observations of Karmic Relationships in 6 Volumes, Vol. 3: The Karmic Relationships of the Anthroposophical Movement
CW 238	Esoteric Observations of Karmic Relationships in 6 Volumes, Vol. 4: The Spiritual Life of the Present in Relationship to the Anthroposophical Movement
CW 239	Esoteric Observations of Karmic Relationships in 6 Volumes, Vol. 5
CW 240	Esoteric Observations of Karmic Relationships in 6 Volumes, Vol. 6
CW 243	The Consciousness of the Initiate
CW 245	Instructions for an Esoteric Schooling
CW 250	The Building-Up of the Anthroposophical Society. From the Beginning to the Outbreak of the First World War
CW 251	The History of the Goetheanum Building-Association
CW 252	Life in the Anthroposophical Society from the First World War to the Burning of the First Goetheanum
CW 253	The Problems of Living Together in the Anthroposophical Society. On the Dornach Crisis of 1915. With Highlights on Swedenborg's Clairvoyance, the Views of Freudian Psychoanalysts, and the Concept of Love in Relation to Mysticism
CW 254	The Occult Movement in the 19th Century and Its Relationship to World Culture. Significant Points from the Exoteric Cultural Life around the Middle of the 19th Century
CW 255	Rudolf Steiner during the First World War
CW 255a	Anthroposophy and the Reformation of Society. On the History of the Threefold Movement

CW 255b	Anthroposophy and Its Opponents, 1919-1921
CW 256	How Can the Anthroposophical Movement Be Financed?
CW 256a	Futurum, Inc. / International Laboratories, Inc.
CW 256b	The Coming Day, Inc.
CW 257	Anthroposophical Community-Building
CW 258	The History of and Conditions for the Anthroposophical Movement in Relationship to the Anthroposophical Society. A Stimulus to Self-Contemplation
CW 259	The Year of Destiny 1923 in the History of the Anthroposophical Society. From the Burning of the Goetheanum to the Christmas Conference
CW 260	The Christmas Conference for the Founding of the General Anthroposophical Society
CW 260a	The Constitution of the General Anthroposophical Society and the School for Spiritual Science. The Rebuilding of the Goetheanum
CW 261	Our Dead. Addresses, Words of Remembrance, and Meditative Verses, 1906-1924
CW 262	Rudolf Steiner and Marie Steiner-von Sivers: Correspondence and Documents, 1901-1925
CW 263/1	Rudolf Steiner and Edith Maryon: Correspondence: Letters, Verses, Sketches, 1912-1924
CW 264	On the History and the Contents of the First Section of the Esoteric School from 1904 to 1914. Letters, Newsletters, Documents, Lectures
CW 265	On the History and from the Contents of the Ritual-Knowledge Section of the Esoteric School from 1904 to 1914. Documents, and Lectures from the Years 1906 to 1914, as Well as on New Approaches to Ritual-Knowledge Work in the Years 1921-1924
CW 266/1	From the Contents of the Esoteric Lessons. Volume 1: 1904-1909. Notes from Memory of Participants. Meditation texts from the notes of Rudolf Steiner
CW 266/2	From the Contents of the Esoteric Lessons. Volume 2: 1910-1912. Notes from Memory of Participants
CW 266/3	From the Contents of the Esoteric Lessons. Volume 3: 1913, 1914 and 1920-1923. Notes from Memory of Participants. Meditation texts from the notes of Rudolf Steiner
CW 267	Soul-Exercises: Vol. 1: Exercises with Word and Image Meditations for the Methodological Development of Higher Powers of Knowledge, 1904-1924
CW 268	Soul-Exercises: Vol. 2: Mantric Verses, 1903-1925
CW 269	Ritual Texts for the Celebration of the Free Christian Religious Instruction. The Collected Verses for Teachers and Students of the Waldorf School
CW 270	Esoteric Instructions for the First Class of the School for Spiritual Science at the Goetheanum 1924, 4 Volumes

III. Lectures and Courses on Specific Realms of Life

Lectures on Art

CW 271 Art and Knowledge of Art. Foundations of a New Aesthetic
CW 272 Spiritual-Scientific Commentary on Goethe's "Faust" in Two Volumes. Vol. 1: Faust, the Striving Human Being
CW 273 Spiritual-Scientific Commentary on Goethe's "Faust" in Two Volumes. Vol. 2: The Faust-Problem
CW 274 Addresses for the Christmas Plays from the Old Folk Traditions
CW 275 Art in the Light of Mystery Wisdom
CW 276 The Artistic in Its Mission in the World. The Genius of Language. The World of Self-Revealing Radiant Appearances – Anthroposophy and Art. Anthroposophy and Poetry
CW 277 Eurythmy. The Revelation of the Speaking Soul
CW 277a The Origin and Development of Eurythmy
CW 278 Eurythmy as Visible Song
CW 279 Eurythmy as Visible Speech
CW 280 The Method and Nature of Speech Formation
CW 281 The Art of Recitation and Declamation
CW 282 Speech Formation and Dramatic Art
CW 283 The Nature of Things Musical and the Experience of Tone in the Human Being
CW 284/285 Images of Occult Seals and Pillars. The Munich Congress of Whitsun 1907 and Its Consequences
CW 286 Paths to a New Style of Architecture. "And the Building Becomes Human"
CW 287 The Building at Dornach as a Symbol of Historical Becoming and an Artistic Transformation Impulse
CW 288 Style-Forms in the Living Organic
CW 289 The Building-Idea of the Goetheanum: Lectures with Slides from the Years 1920-1921
CW 290 The Building-Idea of the Goetheanum: Lectures with Slides from the Years 1920-1921
CW 291 The Nature of Colors
CW 291a Knowledge of Colors. Supplementary Volume to "The Nature of Colors"
CW 292 Art History as Image of Inner Spiritual Impulses

Lectures on Education

CW 293 General Knowledge of the Human Being as the Foundation of Pedagogy
CW 294 The Art of Education, Methodology and Didactics
CW 295 The Art of Education: Seminar Discussions and Lectures on Lesson Planning

CW 296 The Question of Education as a Social Question
CW 297 The Idea and Practice of the Waldorf School
CW 297a Education for Life: Self-Education and the Practice of Pedagogy
CW 298 Rudolf Steiner in the Waldorf School
CW 299 Spiritual-Scientific Observations on Speech
CW 300a Conferences with the Teachers of the Free Waldorf School in Stuttgart, 1919 to 1924, in 3 Volumes, Vol. 1
CW 300b Conferences with the Teachers of the Free Waldorf School in Stuttgart, 1919 to 1924, in 3 Volumes, Vol. 2
CW 300c Conferences with the Teachers of the Free Waldorf School in Stuttgart, 1919 to 1924, in 3 Volumes, Vol. 3
CW 301 The Renewal of Pedagogical-Didactical Art through Spiritual Science
CW 302 Knowledge of the Human Being and the Forming of Class Lessons
CW 302a Education and Teaching from a Knowledge of the Human Being
CW 303 The Healthy Development of the Human Being
CW 304 Methods of Education and Teaching Based on Anthroposophy
CW 304a Anthroposophical Knowledge of the Human Being and Pedagogy
CW 305 The Soul-Spiritual Foundational Forces of the Art of Education. Spiritual Values in Education and Social Life
CW 306 Pedagogical Praxis from the Viewpoint of a Spiritual-Scientific Knowledge of the Human Being. The Education of the Child and Young Human Beings
CW 307 The Spiritual Life of the Present and Education
CW 308 The Method of Teaching and the Life-Requirements for Teaching
CW 309 Anthroposophical Pedagogy and Its Prerequisites
CW 310 The Pedagogical Value of a Knowledge of the Human Being and the Cultural Value of Pedagogy
CW 311 The Art of Education from an Understanding of the Being of Humanity

Lectures on Medicine

CW 312 Spiritual Science and Medicine
CW 313 Spiritual-Scientific Viewpoints on Therapy
CW 314 Physiology and Therapy Based on Spiritual Science
CW 315 Curative Eurythmy
CW 316 Meditative Observations and Instructions for a Deepening of the Art of Healing
CW 317 The Curative Education Course
CW 318 The Working Together of Doctors and Pastors
CW 319 Anthroposophical Knowledge of the Human Being and Medicine

<u>*Lectures on Natural Science*</u>

CW 320 Spiritual-Scientific Impulses for the Development of Physics 1: The First Natural-Scientific Course: Light, Color, Tone, Mass, Electricity, Magnetism
CW 321 Spiritual-Scientific Impulses for the Development of Physics 2: The Second Natural-Scientific Course: Warmth at the Border of Positive and Negative Materiality
CW 322 The Borders of the Knowledge of Nature
CW 323 The Relationship of the various Natural-Scientific Fields to Astronomy
CW 324 Nature Observation, Mathematics, and Scientific Experimentation and Results from the Viewpoint of Anthroposophy
CW 324a The Fourth Dimension in Mathematics and Reality
CW 325 Natural Science and the World-Historical Development of Humanity since Ancient Times
CW 326 The Moment of the Coming Into Being of Natural Science in World History and Its Development Since Then
CW 327 Spiritual-Scientific Foundations for Success in Farming. The Agricultural Course

<u>*Lectures on Social Life and the Threefold Arrangement of the Social Organism*</u>

CW 328 The Social Question
CW 329 The Liberation of the Human Being as the Foundation for a New Social Form
CW 330 The Renewal of the Social Organism
CW 331 Work-Council and Socialization
CW 332 The Alliance for Threefolding and the Total Reform of Society. The Council on Culture and the Liberation of the Spiritual Life
CW 332a The Social Future
CW 333 Freedom of Thought and Social Forces
CW 334 From the Unified State to the Threefold Social Organism
CW 335 The Crisis of the Present and the Path to Healthy Thinking
CW 336 The Great Questions of the Times and Anthroposophical Spiritual Knowledge
CW 337a Social Ideas, Social Reality, Social Practice, Vol. 1: Question-and-Answer Evenings and Study Evenings of the Alliance for the Threefold Social Organism in Stuttgart, 1919-1920
CW 337b Social Ideas, Social Realities, Social Practice, Vol. 2: Discussion Evenings of the Swiss Alliance for the Threefold Social Organism
CW 338 How Does One Work on Behalf of the Impulse for the Threefold Social Organism?
CW 339 Anthroposophy, Threefold Social Organism, and the Art of Public Speaking

SIGNIFICANT EVENTS IN THE LIFE OF RUDOLF STEINER

1829: June 23: birth of Johann Steiner (1829-1910)—Rudolf Steiner's father—in Geras, Lower Austria.

1834: May 8: birth of Franciska Blie (1834-1918)—Rudolf Steiner's mother—in Horn, Lower Austria. "My father and mother were both children of the glorious Lower Austrian forest district north of the Danube."

1860: May 16: marriage of Johann Steiner and Franciska Blie.

1861: February 25: birth of *Rudolf Joseph Lorenz Steiner* in Kraljevec, Croatia, near the border with Hungary, where Johann Steiner works as a telegrapher for the South Austria Railroad. Rudolf Steiner is baptized two days later, February 27, the date usually given as his birthday.

1862: Summer: the family moves to Mödling, Lower Austria.

1863: The family moves to Pottschach, Lower Austria, near the Styrian border, where Johann Steiner becomes stationmaster. "The view stretched to the mountains...majestic peaks in the distance and the sweet charm of nature in the immediate surroundings."

1864: November 15: birth of Rudolf Steiner's sister, Leopoldine (d. November 1, 1927). She will become a seamstress and live with her parents for the rest of her life.

1866: July 28: birth of Rudolf Steiner's deaf-mute brother, Gustav (d. May 1, 1941).

1867: Rudolf Steiner enters the village school. Following a disagreement between his father and the schoolmaster, whose wife falsely accused the boy of causing a commotion, Rudolf Steiner is taken out of school and taught at home.

1868: A critical experience. Unknown to the family, an aunt dies in a distant town. Sitting in the station waiting room, Rudolf Steiner sees her "form," which speaks to him, asking for help. "Beginning with this experience, a new soul life began in the boy, one in which not only the outer trees and mountains spoke to him, but also the worlds that lay behind them. From this moment on, the boy began to live with the spirits of nature...."

1869: The family moves to the peaceful, rural village of Neudorfl, near Wiener-Neustadt in present-day Austria. Rudolf Steiner attends the village school. Because of the "unorthodoxy" of his writing and spelling, he has to do "extra lessons."

1870: Through a book lent to him by his tutor, he discovers geometry: "To grasp something purely in the spirit brought me inner happiness. I know that I first learned happiness through geometry." The same tutor allows him to draw, while other students still struggle with their reading and writing. "An artistic element" thus enters his education.

1871: Though his parents are not religious, Rudolf Steiner becomes a "church child," a favorite of the priest, who was "an exceptional character." "Up to the age of ten or eleven, among those I came to know, he was far and away the most significant." Among other things, he introduces Steiner to Copernican, heliocentric cosmology. As an altar boy, Rudolf Steiner serves at Masses, funerals, and Corpus Christi processions. At year's end, after an incident in which he escapes a thrashing, his father forbids him to go to church.

1872: Rudolf Steiner transfers to grammar school in Wiener-Neustadt, a five-mile walk from home, which must be done in all weathers.

1873-75: Through his teachers and on his own, Rudolf Steiner has many wonderful experiences with science and mathematics. Outside school, he teaches himself analytic geometry, trigonometry, differential equations, and calculus.

1876: Rudolf Steiner begins tutoring other students. He learns bookbinding from his father. He also teaches himself stenography.

1877: Rudolf Steiner discovers Kant's *Critique of Pure Reason*, which he reads and rereads. He also discovers and reads von Rotteck's *World History*.

1878: He studies extensively in contemporary psychology and philosophy.

1879: Rudolf Steiner graduates from high school with honors. His father is transferred to Inzersdorf, near Vienna. He uses his first visit to Vienna "to purchase a great number of philosophy books"—Kant, Fichte, Schelling, and Hegel, as well as numerous histories of philosophy. His aim: to find a path from the "I" to nature.

October 1879-1883: Rudolf Steiner attends the Technical College in Vienna—to study mathematics, chemistry, physics, mineralogy, botany, zoology, biology, geology, and mechanics—with a scholarship. He also attends lectures in history and literature, while avidly reading philosophy on his own. His two favorite professors are Karl Julius Schröer (German language and literature) and Edmund Reitlinger (physics). He also audits lectures by Robert Zimmerman on aesthetics and Franz Brentano on philosophy. During this year he begins his friendship with Moritz Zitter (1861-1921), who will help support him financially when he is in Berlin.

1880: Rudolf Steiner attends lectures on Schiller and Goethe by Karl Julius Schröer, who becomes his mentor. Also "through a remarkable combination of circumstances," he meets Felix Koguzki, an "herb gatherer" and healer, who could "see deeply into the secrets of nature." Rudolf Steiner will meet and study with this "emissary of the Master" throughout his time in Vienna.

1881: January: "... I didn't sleep a wink. I was busy with philosophical problems until about 12:30 a.m. Then, finally, I threw myself down on my couch. All my striving during the previous year had been to research whether the following statement by Schelling was true or not: *Within everyone dwells a secret, marvelous capacity to draw back from the stream of time—out of the self clothed in all that comes to us from outside—into our innermost being and there, in the immutable form of the Eternal, to look into ourselves.* I believe, and I am still quite certain of it, that I discovered this capacity in myself; I had long had an inkling of it. Now the whole of idealist philosophy stood before me in modified form. What's a sleepless night compared to that!"

Rudolf Steiner begins communicating with leading thinkers of the day, who send him books in return, which he reads eagerly.

July: "I am not one of those who dives into the day like an animal in human form. I pursue a quite specific goal, an idealistic aim—knowledge of the truth! This cannot be done offhandedly. It requires the greatest striving in the world, free of all egotism, and equally of all resignation."

August: Steiner puts down on paper for the first time thoughts for a "Philosophy of Freedom." "The striving for the absolute: this human yearning is freedom." He also seeks to outline a "peasant philosophy," describing what the worldview of a "peasant"—one who lives close to the earth and the old ways—really is.

1881-1882: Felix Koguzki, the herb gatherer, reveals himself to be the envoy of another, higher initiatory personality, who instructs Rudolf Steiner to penetrate Fichte's philosophy and to master modern scientific thinking as a preparation for right entry into the spirit. This "Master" also teaches him the double (evolutionary and involutionary) nature of time.

1882: Through the offices of Karl Julius Schröer, Rudolf Steiner is asked by Joseph Kurschner to edit Goethe's scientific works for the *Deutschen National-Literatur* edition. He writes "A Possible Critique of Atomistic Concepts" and sends it to Friedrich Theodore Vischer.

1883: Rudolf Steiner completes his college studies and begins work on the Goethe project.

1884: First volume of Goethe's *Scientific Writings* (CW 1) appears (March). He lectures on Goethe and Lessing, and Goethe's approach to science. In July, he enters the household of Ladislaus and Pauline Specht as tutor to the four Specht boys. He will live there until 1890. At this time, he meets Josef Breuer (1842-1925), the coauthor with Sigmund Freud of *Studies in Hysteria*, who is the Specht family doctor.

1885: While continuing to edit Goethe's writings, Rudolf Steiner reads deeply in contemporary philosophy (Edouard von Hartmann, Johannes Volkelt, and Richard Wahle, among others).

1886: May: Rudolf Steiner sends Kurschner the manuscript of *Outlines of Goethe's Theory of Knowledge* (CW 2), which appears in October, and which he sends out widely. He also meets the poet Marie Eugenie Delle Grazie and writes "Nature and Our Ideals" for her. He attends her salon, where he meets many priests, theologians, and philosophers, who will become his friends. Meanwhile, the director of the Goethe Archive in Weimar requests his collaboration with the *Sophien* edition of Goethe's works, particularly the writings on color.

1887: At the beginning of the year, Rudolf Steiner is very sick. As the year progresses and his health improves, he becomes increasingly "a man of letters," lecturing, writing essays, and taking part in Austrian cultural life. In August-September, the second volume of Goethe's *Scientific Writings* appears.

1888: January-July: Rudolf Steiner assumes editorship of the "German Weekly" (*Deutsche Wochenschrift*). He begins lecturing more intensively, giving, for example, a lecture titled "Goethe as Father of a New Aesthetics." He meets and becomes soul friends with Friedrich Eckstein (1861-1939), a vegetarian, philosopher of symbolism, alchemist, and musician, who will introduce him to various spiritual currents (including theosophy) and with whom he will meditate and interpret esoteric and alchemical texts.

1889: Rudolf Steiner first reads Nietzsche (*Beyond Good and Evil*). He encounters Theosophy again and learns of Madame Blavatsky in the Theosophical circle around Marie Lang (1858-1934). Here he also meets well-known figures of Austrian life, as well as esoteric figures like the occultist Franz Hartman and Karl Leinigen-Billigen (translator of C.G. Harrison's *The Transcendental Universe*.) During this period, Steiner first reads A.P. Sinnett's *Esoteric Buddhism* and Mabel Collins's *Light on the Path*. He also begins traveling, visiting Budapest, Weimar, and Berlin (where he meets philosopher Edouard von Hartman).

1890: Rudolf Steiner finishes volume 3 of Goethe's scientific writings. He begins his doctoral dissertation, which will become *Truth and Science* (CW 3). He also meets the poet and feminist Rosa Mayreder (1858-1938), with whom he can exchange his most intimate thoughts. In September, Rudolf Steiner moves to Weimar to work in the Goethe-Schiller Archive.

1891: Volume 3 of the Kurschner edition of Goethe appears. Meanwhile, Rudolf Steiner edits Goethe's studies in mineralogy and scientific writings for the *Sophien* edition. He meets Ludwig Laistner of the Cotta Publishing Company, who asks for a book on the basic question of metaphysics. From this will result, ultimately, *The Philosophy of Freedom* (CW 4), which will be published not by Cotta but by Emil Felber. In October, Rudolf Steiner takes the oral exam for a doctorate in philosophy, mathematics, and mechanics at Rostock University, receiving his doctorate on the twenty-sixth. In November, he gives his first lecture on Goethe's "Fairy Tale" in Vienna.

1892: Rudolf Steiner continues work at the Goethe-Schiller Archive and on his *Philosophy of Freedom*. *Truth and Science*, his doctoral dissertation, is published. Steiner undertakes to write introductions to books on Schopenhauer and Jean Paul for Cotta. At year's end, he finds lodging with Anna Eunike, née Schulz (1853-1911), a widow with four daughters and a son. He also develops a friendship with Otto Erich Hartleben (1864-1905) with whom he shares literary interests.

1893: Rudolf Steiner begins his habit of producing many reviews and articles. In March, he gives a lecture titled "Hypnotism, with Reference to Spiritism." In September, volume 4 of the Kurschner edition is completed. In November, *The Philosophy of Freedom* appears. This year, too, he meets John Henry Mackay (1864-1933), the anarchist, and Max Stirner, a scholar and biographer.

1894: Rudolf Steiner meets Elisabeth Förster Nietzsche, the philosopher's sister, and begins to read Nietzsche in earnest, beginning with the as yet unpublished *Antichrist.* He also meets Ernst Haeckel (1834-1919). In the fall, he begins to write *Nietzsche, A Fighter against His Time* (CW 5).

1895: May, *Nietzsche, A Fighter against His Time* appears.

1896: January 22: Rudolf Steiner sees Friedrich Nietzsche for the first and only time. Moves between the Nietzsche and the Goethe-Schiller Archives, where he completes his work before year's end. He falls out with Elisabeth Förster Nietzsche, thus ending his association with the Nietzsche Archive.

1897: Rudolf Steiner finishes the manuscript of *Goethe's Worldview* (CW 6). He moves to Berlin with Anna Eunike and begins editorship of the *Magazin fur Literatur.* From now on, Steiner will write countless reviews, literary and philosophical articles, and so on. He begins lecturing at the "Free Literary Society." In September, he attends the Zionist Congress in Basel. He sides with Dreyfus in the Dreyfus affair.

1898: Rudolf Steiner is very active as an editor in the political, artistic, and theatrical life of Berlin. He becomes friendly with John Henry Mackay and poet Ludwig Jacobowski (1868-1900). He joins Jacobowski's circle of writers, artists, and scientists—"The Coming Ones" (*Die Kommenden*)—and contributes lectures to the group until 1903. He also lectures at the "League for College Pedagogy." He writes an article for Goethe's sesquicentennial, "Goethe's Secret Revelation," on the "Fairy Tale of the Green Snake and the Beautiful Lily."

1898-99: "This was a trying time for my soul as I looked at Christianity.... I was able to progress only by contemplating, by means of spiritual perception, the evolution of Christianity .... Conscious knowledge of real Christianity began to dawn in me around the turn of the century. This seed continued to develop. My soul trial occurred shortly before the beginning of the twentieth century. It was decisive for my soul's development that I stood spiritually before the Mystery of Golgotha in a deep and solemn celebration of knowledge."

1899: Rudolf Steiner begins teaching and giving lectures and lecture cycles at the Workers' College, founded by Wilhelm Liebknecht (1826-1900). He will continue to do so until 1904. Writes: *Literature and Spiritual Life in the Nineteenth Century; Individualism in Philosophy; Haeckel and His Opponents; Poetry in the Present;* and begins what will become (fifteen years later). *The Riddles of Philosophy* (CW 18). He also meets many artists and writers, including Käthe Kollwitz, Stefan

Zweig, and Rainer Maria Rilke. On October 31, he marries Anna Eunike.

1900: "I thought that the turn of the century must bring humanity a new light. It seemed to me that the separation of human thinking and willing from the spirit had peaked. A turn or reversal of direction in human evolution seemed to me a necessity." Rudolf Steiner finishes *World and Life Views in the Nineteenth Century* (the second part of what will become *The Riddles of Philosophy*) and dedicates it to Ernst Haeckel. It is published in March. He continues lecturing at *Die Kommenden*, whose leadership he assumes after the death of Jacobowski. Also, he gives the Gutenberg Jubilee lecture before 7,000 typesetters and printers. In September, Rudolf Steiner is invited by Count and Countess Brockdorff to lecture in the Theosophical Library. His first lecture is on Nietzsche. His second lecture is titled "Goethe's Secret Revelation." October 6, he begins a lecture cycle on the mystics that will become *Mystics after Modernism* (CW 7). November-December: "Marie von Sivers appears in the audience...." Also in November, Steiner gives his first lecture at the Giordano Bruno Bund (where he will continue to lecture until May, 1905). He speaks on Bruno and modern Rome, focusing on the importance of the philosophy of Thomas Aquinas as monism.

1901: In continual financial straits, Rudolf Steiner's early friends Moritz Zitter and Rosa Mayreder help support him. In October, he begins the lecture cycle *Christianity as Mystical Fact* (CW 8) at the Theosophical Library. In November, he gives his first "Theosophical lecture" on Goethe's "Fairy Tale" in Hamburg at the invitation of Wilhelm Hubbe-Schleiden. He also attends a tea to celebrate the founding of the Theosophical Society at Count and Countess Brockdorff's. He gives a lecture cycle, "From Buddha to Christ," for the circle of the *Kommenden*. November 17, Marie von Sivers asks Rudolf Steiner if Theosophy does not need a Western-Christian spiritual movement (to complement Theosophy's Eastern emphasis). "The question was posed. Now, following spiritual laws, I could begin to give an answer...." In December, Rudolf Steiner writes his first article for a Theosophical publication. At year's end, the Brockdorffs and possibly Wilhelm Hubbe-Schleiden ask Rudolf Steiner to join the Theosophical Society and undertake the leadership of the German Section. Rudolf Steiner agrees, on the condition that Marie von Sivers (then in Italy) work with him.

1902: Beginning in January, Rudolf Steiner attends the opening of the Workers' School in Spandau with Rosa Luxemberg (1870-1919). January 17, Rudolf Steiner joins the Theosophical Society. In April, he is asked to become general secretary of the German Section of the Theosophical Society, and works on preparations for its founding. In July, he visits London for a Theosophical congress. He meets Bertram

Keightly, G.R.S. Mead, A.P. Sinnett, and Annie Besant, among others. In September, *Christianity as Mystical Fact* appears. In October, Rudolf Steiner gives his first public lecture on theosophy ("Monism and Theosophy") to about three hundred people at the Giordano Bruno Bund. On October 19-21, the German Section of the Theosophical Society has its first meeting; Rudolf Steiner is the general secretary, and Annie Besant attends. Steiner lectures on practical karma studies. On October 23, Annie Besant inducts Rudolf Steiner into the Esoteric School of the Theosophical Society. On October 25, Steiner begins a weekly series of lectures: "The Field of Theosophy." During this year, Rudolf Steiner also first meets Ita Wegman (1876-1943), who will become his close collaborator in his final years.

1903: Rudolf Steiner holds about 300 lectures and seminars. In May, the first issue of the periodical *Luzifer* appears. In June, Rudolf Steiner visits London for the first meeting of the Federation of the European Sections of the Theosophical Society, where he meets Colonel Olcott. He begins to write *Theosophy* (CW 9).

1904: Rudolf Steiner continues lecturing at the Workers' College and elsewhere (about 90 lectures), while lecturing intensively all over Germany among Theosophists (about a 140 lectures). In February, he meets Carl Unger (1878-1929), who will become a member of the board of the Anthroposophical Society (1913). In March, he meets Michael Bauer (1871-1929), a Christian mystic, who will also be on the board. In May, *Theosophy* appears, with the dedication: "To the spirit of Giordano Bruno." Rudolf Steiner and Marie von Sivers visit London for meetings with Annie Besant. June: Rudolf Steiner and Marie von Sivers attend the meeting of the Federation of European Sections of the Theosophical Society in Amsterdam. In July, Steiner begins the articles in *Luzifer-Gnosis* that will become *How to Know Higher Worlds* (CW 10) and *Cosmic Memory* (CW 11). In September, Annie Besant visits Germany. In December, Steiner lectures on Freemasonry. He mentions the High Grade Masonry derived from John Yarker and represented by Theodore Reuss and Karl Kellner as a blank slate "into which a good image could be placed."

1905: This year, Steiner ends his non-Theosophical lecturing activity. Supported by Marie von Sivers, his Theosophical lecturing—both in public and in the Theosophical Society—increases significantly: "The German Theosophical Movement is of exceptional importance." Steiner recommends reading, among others, Fichte, Jacob Boehme, and Angelus Silesius. He begins to introduce Christian themes into Theosophy. He also begins to work with doctors (Felix Peipers and Ludwig Noll). In July, he is in London for the Federation of European Sections, where he attends a lecture by Annie Besant: "I have seldom seen Mrs. Besant speak in so inward and heartfelt a manner...." "Through Mrs. Besant I have found the way to H.P. Blavatsky."

September to October, he gives a course of thirty-one lectures for a small group of esoteric students. In October, the annual meeting of the German Section of the Theosophical Society, which still remains very small, takes place. Rudolf Steiner reports membership has risen from 121 to 377 members. In November, seeking to establish esoteric "continuity," Rudolf Steiner and Marie von Sivers participate in a "Memphis-Misraim" Masonic ceremony. They pay forty-five marks for membership. "Yesterday, you saw how little remains of former esoteric institutions." "We are dealing only with a 'framework'... for the present, nothing lies behind it. The occult powers have completely withdrawn."

1906: Expansion of Theosophical work. Rudolf Steiner gives about 245 lectures, only 44 of which take place in Berlin. Cycles are given in Paris, Leipzig, Stuttgart, and Munich. Esoteric work also intensifies. Rudolf Steiner begins writing *An Outline of Esoteric Science* (CW 13). In January, Rudolf Steiner receives permission (a patent) from the Great Orient of the Scottish A & A Thirty-Three Degree Rite of the Order of the Ancient Freemasons of the Memphis-Misraim Rite to direct a chapter under the name "Mystica Aeterna." This will become the "Cognitive Cultic Section" (also called "Misraim Service") of the Esoteric School. (See: *From the History and Contents of the Cognitive Cultic Section* (CW 264). During this time, Steiner also meets Albert Schweitzer. In May, he is in Paris, where he visits Edouard Schuré. Many Russians attend his lectures (including Konstantin Balmont, Dimitri Mereszkovski, Zinaida Hippius, and Maximilian Woloshin). He attends the General Meeting of the European Federation of the Theosophical Society, at which Col. Olcott is present for the last time. He spends the year's end in Venice and Rome, where he writes and works on his translation of H.P. Blavatsky's *Key to Theosophy*.

1907: Further expansion of the German Theosophical Movement according to the Rosicrucian directive to "introduce spirit into the world"—in education, in social questions, in art, and in science. In February, Col. Olcott dies in Adyar. Before he dies, Olcott indicates that "the Masters" wish Annie Besant to succeed him: much politicking ensues. Rudolf Steiner supports Besant's candidacy. April-May: preparations for the Congress of the Federation of European Sections of the Theosophical Society—the great, watershed Whitsun "Munich Congress," attended by Annie Besant and others. Steiner decides to separate Eastern and Western (Christian-Rosicrucian) esoteric schools. He takes his esoteric school out of the Theosophical Society (Besant and Rudolf Steiner are "in harmony" on this). Steiner makes his first lecture tours to Austria and Hungary. That summer, he is in Italy. In September, he visits Edouard Schuré, who will write the introduction to the French edition of *Christianity as Mystical Fact* in Barr, Alsace. Rudolf Steiner writes the autobiographical statement known as the "Barr Document." In *Luzifer–Gnosis*, "The Education of the Child" appears.

1908: The movement grows (membership: 1150). Lecturing expands. Steiner makes his first extended lecture tour to Holland and Scandinavia, as well as visits to Naples and Sicily. Themes: St. John's Gospel, the Apocalypse, Egypt, science, philosophy, and logic. *Luzifer-Gnosis* ceases publication. In Berlin, Marie von Sivers (with Johanna Mücke (1864-1949) forms the *Philosophisch-Theosophisch* (after 1915 *Philosophisch-Anthroposophisch*) *Verlag* to publish Steiner's work. Steiner gives lecture cycles titled *The Gospel of St. John* (CW 103) and *The Apocalypse* (104).

1909: *An Outline of Esoteric Science* appears. Lecturing and travel continues. Rudolf Steiner's spiritual research expands to include the polarity of Lucifer and Ahriman; the work of great individualities in history; the Maitreya Buddha and the Bodhisattvas; spiritual economy (CW 109); the work of the spiritual hierarchies in heaven and on Earth (CW 110). He also deepens and intensifies his research into the Gospels, giving lectures on the Gospel of St. Luke (CW 114) with the first mention of two Jesus children. Meets and becomes friends with Christian Morgenstern (1871-1914). In April, he lays the foundation stone for the Malsch model—the building that will lead to the first Goetheanum. In May, the International Congress of the Federation of European Sections of the Theosophical Society takes place in Budapest. Rudolf Steiner receives the Subba Row medal for *How to Know Higher Worlds*. During this time, Charles W. Leadbeater discovers Jiddu Krishnamurti (1895-1986) and proclaims him the future "world teacher," the bearer of the Maitreya Buddha and the "reappearing Christ." In October, Steiner delivers seminal lectures on "anthroposophy," which he will try, unsuccessfully, to rework over the next years into the unfinished work, *Anthroposophy (A Fragment)* (CW 45).

1910: New themes: *The Reappearance of Christ in the Etheric* (CW 118); *The Fifth Gospel; The Mission of Folk Souls* (CW 121); *Occult History* (CW 126); the evolving development of etheric cognitive capacities. Rudolf Steiner continues his Gospel research with *The Gospel of St. Matthew* (CW 123). In January, his father dies. In April, he takes a month-long trip to Italy, including Rome, Monte Cassino, and Sicily. He also visits Scandinavia again. July-August, he writes the first mystery drama, *The Portal of Initiation* (CW 14). In November, he gives "psychosophy" lectures. In December, he submits "On the Psychological Foundations and Epistemological Framework of Theosophy" to the International Philosophical Congress in Bologna.

1911: The crisis in the Theosophical Society deepens. In January, "The Order of the Rising Sun," which will soon become "The Order of the Star in the East," is founded for the coming world teacher, Krishnamurti. At the same time, Marie von Sivers, Rudolf Steiner's coworker, falls ill. Fewer lectures are given, but important new ground is broken. In Prague, in March, Steiner meets Franz Kafka (1883-1924) and Hugo Bergmann (1883-1975). In April, he delivers his paper to the

Philosophical Congress. He writes the second mystery drama, *The Soul's Probation* (CW 14). Also, while Marie von Sivers is convalescing, Rudolf Steiner begins work on *Calendar 1912/1913*, which will contain the "Calendar of the Soul" meditations. On March 19, Anna (Eunike) Steiner dies. In September, Rudolf Steiner visits Einsiedeln, birthplace of Paracelsus. In December, Friedrich Rittelmeyer, future founder of the Christian Community, meets Rudolf Steiner. The *Johannes-Bauverein*, the "building committee," which would lead to the first Goetheanum (first planned for Munich), is also founded, and a preliminary committee for the founding of an independent association is created that, in the following year, will become the Anthroposophical Society. Important lecture cycles include *Occult Physiology* (CW 128); *Wonders of the World* (CW 129); *From Jesus to Christ* (CW 131). Other themes: esoteric Christianity; Christian Rosenkreutz; the spiritual guidance of humanity; the sense world and the world of the spirit.

1912: Despite the ongoing, now increasing crisis in the Theosophical Society, much is accomplished: *Calendar 1912/1913* is published; eurythmy is created; both the third mystery drama, *The Guardian of the Threshold* (CW 14) and *A Way of Self-Knowledge* (CW 16) are written. New (or renewed) themes included life between death and rebirth and karma and reincarnation. Other lecture cycles: *Spiritual Beings in the Heavenly Bodies and the Kingdoms of Nature* (CW 136); *The Human Being in the Light of Occultism, Theosophy, and Philosophy* (CW 137); *The Gospel of St. Mark* (CW 139); and *The Bhagavad Gita and the Epistles of Paul* (CW 142). On May 8, Rudolf Steiner celebrates White Lotus Day, H.P. Blavatsky's death day, which he had faithfully observed for the past decade, for the last time. In August, Rudolf Steiner suggests the "independent association" be called the "Anthroposophical Society." In September, the first eurythmy course takes place. In October, Rudolf Steiner declines recognition of a Theosophical Society lodge dedicated to the Star of the East and decides to expel all Theosophical Society members belonging to the order. Also, with Marie von Sivers, he first visits Dornach, near Basel, Switzerland, and they stand on the hill where the Goetheanum will be. In November, a Theosophical Society lodge is opened by direct mandate from Adyar (Annie Besant). In December, a meeting of the German section occurs at which it is decided that belonging to the Order of the Star of the East is incompatible with membership in the Theosophical Society. December 28: informal founding of the Anthroposophical Society in Berlin.

1913: Expulsion of the German section from the Theosophical Society. February 2-3: Foundation meeting of the Anthroposophical Society. Board members include: Marie von Sivers, Michael Bauer, and Carl Unger. September 20: Laying of the foundation stone for the *Johannes Bau* (Goetheanum) in Dornach. Building begins immediately. The third mystery drama, *The Soul's Awakening* (CW 14), is completed.

Also: *The Threshold of the Spiritual World* (CW 147). Lecture cycles include: *The Bhagavad Gita and the Epistles of Paul* and *The Esoteric Meaning of the Bhagavad Gita* (CW 146), which the Russian philosopher Nikolai Berdyaev attends; *The Mysteries of the East and of Christianity* (CW 144); *The Effects of Esoteric Development* (CW 145); and *The Fifth Gospel* (CW 148). In May, Rudolf Steiner is in London and Paris, where anthroposophical work continues.

1914: Building continues on the *Johannes Bau* (Goetheanum) in Dornach, with artists and coworkers from seventeen nations. The general assembly of the Anthroposophical Society takes place. In May, Rudolf Steiner visits Paris, as well as Chartres Cathedral. June 28: assassination in Sarajevo ("Now the catastrophe has happened!"). August 1: War is declared. Rudolf Steiner returns to Germany from Dornach—he will travel back and forth. He writes the last chapter of *The Riddles of Philosophy*. Lecture cycles include: *Human and Cosmic Thought* (CW 151); *Inner Being of Humanity between Death and a New Birth* (CW 153); *Occult Reading and Occult Hearing* (CW 156). December 24: marriage of Rudolf Steiner and Marie von Sivers.

1915: Building continues. Life after death becomes a major theme, also art. Writes: *Thoughts during a Time of War* (CW 24). Lectures include: *The Secret of Death* (CW 159); *The Uniting of Humanity through the Christ Impulse* (CW 165).

1916: Rudolf Steiner begins work with Edith Maryon (1872-1924) on the sculpture "The Representative of Humanity" ("The Group"—Christ, Lucifer, and Ahriman). He also works with the alchemist Alexander von Bernus on the quarterly *Das Reich*. He writes *The Riddle of Humanity* (CW 20). Lectures include: *Necessity and Freedom in World History and Human Action* (CW 166); *Past and Present in the Human Spirit* (CW 167); *The Karma of Vocation* (CW 172); *The Karma of Untruthfulness* (CW 173).

1917: Russian Revolution. The U.S. enters the war. Building continues. Rudolf Steiner delineates the idea of the "threefold nature of the human being" (in a public lecture March 15) and the "threefold nature of the social organism" (hammered out in May-June with the help of Otto von Lerchenfeld and Ludwig Polzer-Hoditz in the form of two documents titled *Memoranda*, which were distributed in high places). August-September: Rudolf Steiner writes *The Riddles of the Soul* (CW 20). Also: commentary on "The Chemical Wedding of Christian Rosenkreutz" for Alexander Bernus (*Das Reich*). Lectures include: *The Karma of Materialism* (CW 176); *The Spiritual Background of the Outer World: The Fall of the Spirits of Darkness* (CW 177).

1918: March 18: peace treaty of Brest-Litovsk—"Now everything will truly enter chaos! What is needed is cultural renewal." June: Rudolf Steiner visits Karlstein (Grail) Castle outside Prague. Lecture cycle: *From Symptom to Reality in Modern History* (CW 185). In mid-November,

Emil Molt, of the Waldorf-Astoria Cigarette Company, has the idea of founding a school for his workers' children.

1919: Focus on the threefold social organism: tireless travel, countless lectures, meetings, and publications. At the same time, a new public stage of Anthroposophy emerges as cultural renewal begins. The coming years will see initiatives in pedagogy, medicine, pharmacology, and agriculture. January 27: threefold meeting: " We must first of all, with the money we have, found free schools that can bring people what they need." February: first public eurythmy performance in Zurich. Also: "Appeal to the German People" (CW 24), circulated March 6 as a newspaper insert. In April, *Toward Social Renewal* (CW 23)—"perhaps the most widely read of all books on politics appearing since the war"—appears. Rudolf Steiner is asked to undertake the "direction and leadership" of the school founded by the Waldorf-Astoria Company. Rudolf Steiner begins to talk about the "renewal" of education. May 30: a building is selected and purchased for the future Waldorf School. August-September, Rudolf Steiner gives a lecture course for Waldorf teachers, *The Foundations of Human Experience (Study of Man)* (CW 293). September 7: Opening of the first Waldorf School. December (into January): first science course, the *Light Course* (CW 320).

1920: The Waldorf School flourishes. New threefold initiatives. Founding of limited companies *Der Kommenden Tag* and *Futurum A.G.* to infuse spiritual values into the economic realm. Rudolf Steiner also focuses on the sciences. Lectures: *Introducing Anthroposophical Medicine* (CW 312); *The Warmth Course* (CW 321); *The Boundaries of Natural Science* (CW 322); *The Redemption of Thinking* (CW 74). February: Johannes Werner Klein—later a cofounder of the Christian Community—asks Rudolf Steiner about the possibility of a "religious renewal," a "Johannine church." In March, Rudolf Steiner gives the first course for doctors and medical students. In April, a divinity student asks Rudolf Steiner a second time about the possibility of religious renewal. September 27-October 16: anthroposophical "university course." December: lectures titled *The Search for the New Isis* (CW 202).

1921: Rudolf Steiner continues his intensive work on cultural renewal, including the uphill battle for the threefold social order. "University" arts, scientific, theological, and medical courses include: *The Astronomy Course* (CW 323); *Observation, Mathematics, and Scientific Experiment* (CW 324); the *Second Medical Course* (CW 313); *Color.* In June and September-October, Rudolf Steiner also gives the first two "priests' courses" (CW 342 and 343). The "youth movement" gains momentum. Magazines are founded: *Die Drei* (January), and—under the editorship of Albert Steffen (1884-1963)—the weekly, *Das Goetheanum* (August). In February-March, Rudolf Steiner takes his first trip outside Germany since the war (Holland). On April 7, Steiner receives a letter regarding "religious renewal," and May 22-23, he agrees to address the question in a practical way. In June, the Klinical-Therapeutic Institute opens in Arlesheim under the direction of Dr. Ita Wegman. In August, the Chemical-Pharmaceutical Laboratory opens in Arlesheim (Oskar Schmiedel and Ita Wegman, directors). The Clinical Therapeutic Institute is inaugurated in Stuttgart (Dr. Ludwig Noll, director); also the Research Laboratory in Dornach (Ehrenfried Pfeiffer and Gunther Wachsmuth, directors). In November-December, Rudolf Steiner visits Norway.

1922: The first half of the year involves very active public lecturing (thousands attend); in the second half, Rudolf Steiner begins to withdraw and turn toward the Society—"The Society is asleep." It is "too weak" to do what is asked of it. The businesses—*Die Kommenden Tag* and *Futura A.G.*—fail. In January, with the help of an agent, Steiner undertakes a twelve-city German tour, accompanied by eurythmy performances. In two weeks he speaks to more than 2,000 people. In April, he gives a "university course" in The Hague. He also visits England. In June, he is in Vienna for the East-West Congress. In August-September, he is back in England for the Oxford Conference on Education. Returning to Dornach, he gives the lectures *Philosophy, Cosmology, and Religion* (CW 215), and gives the third priest's course (CW 344). On September 16, The Christian Community is founded. In October-November, Steiner is in Holland and England. He also speaks to the youth: *The Youth Course* (CW 217). In December, Steiner gives lectures titled *The Origins of Natural Science* (CW 326), and *Humanity and the World of Stars: The Spiritual Communion of Humanity* (CW 219). December 31: Fire at the Goetheanum, which is destroyed.

1923: Despite the fire, Rudolf Steiner continues his work unabated. A very hard year. Internal dispersion, dissension, and apathy abound. There is conflict—between old and new visions—within the society. A wake-up call is needed, and Rudolf Steiner responds with renewed lecturing vitality. His focus: the spiritual context of human life; initiation science; the course of the year; and community building. As a foundation for an artistic school, he creates a series of pastel sketches. Lecture cycles: *The Anthroposophical Movement; Initiation Science* (CW 227) (in England at the Penmaenmawr Summer School); *The Four Seasons and the Archangels* (CW 229); *Harmony of the Creative Word* (CW 230); *The Supersensible Human* (CW 231), given in Holland for the founding of the Dutch society. On November 10, in response to the failed Hitler-Ludendorf putsch in Munich, Steiner closes his Berlin residence and moves the *Philosophisch-Anthroposophisch Verlag* (Press) to Dornach. On December 9, Steiner begins the serialization of his *Autobiography: The Course of My Life* (CW 28) in *Das Goetheanum*. It will continue to appear weekly, without a break, until his death. Late December-early January: Rudolf Steiner refounds the Anthroposophical Society (about 12,000 members internationally) and takes over its leadership. The new board members are: Marie Steiner, Ita Wegman, Albert Steffen, Elizabeth Vreede, and Guenther Wachsmuth. (See *The Christmas Meeting for the Founding of the General Anthroposophical Society* (CW 260). Accompanying lectures: *Mystery Knowledge and Mystery Centers* (CW 232); *World History in the Light of Anthroposophy* (CW 233). December 25: the Foundation Stone is laid (in the hearts of members) in the form of the "Foundation Stone Meditation."

1924: January 1: having founded the Anthroposophical Society and taken over its leadership, Rudolf Steiner has the task of "reforming" it. The process begins with a weekly newssheet ("What's Happening in the Anthroposophical Society") in which Rudolf Steiner's "Letters to Members" and "Anthroposophical Leading Thoughts" appear (CW 26). The next step is the creation of a new esoteric class, the "first class" of the "University of Spiritual Science" (which was to have been followed, had Rudolf Steiner lived longer, by two more advanced classes). Then comes a new language for Anthroposophy—practical, phenomenological, and direct; and Rudolf Steiner creates the model for the second Goetheanum. He begins the series of extensive "karma" lectures (CW 235-40); and finally, responding to needs, he creates two new initiatives: biodynamic agriculture and curative education. After the middle of the year, rumors begin to circulate regarding Steiner's health. Lectures: January-February, *Anthroposophy* (CW 234); February: *Tone Eurythmy* (CW 278); June: *The Agriculture Course* (CW 327); June-July: Speech [?] Eurythmy (CW 279); *Curative Education* (CW 317); August: (England, "Second International Summer School"), *Initiation Consciousness: True and False Paths in Spiritual Investigation* (CW 243); September: *Pastoral Medicine* (CW 318). On September 26, for the first time, Rudolf Steiner cancels a lecture. On September 28, he gives his last lecture. On September 29, he withdraws to his studio in the carpenter's shop; now he is definitively ill. Cared for by Ita Wegman, he continues working, however, and writing the weekly installments of his *Autobiography* and *Letters to the Members/Leading Thoughts* (CW 26).

1925: Rudolf Steiner, while continuing to work, continues to weaken. He finishes *Extending Practical Medicine* (CW 27) with Ita Wegman. On March 30, around ten in the morning, Rudolf Steiner dies.

ALPHABETICAL INDEX OF FIRST LINES